Jacqueline Widmar Stewart

Parks and Gardens in Greater Paris

Edition Axel Menges

© 2012 Edition Axel Menges, Stuttgart / London
ISBN 978-3-936681-51-2

Printing and binding: Graspo CZ, a. s., Zlín, Czech
Republic

Editing: Nora Krehl-von Mühlendahl
Design: Axel Menges

Jacket photo: Park of the Château de Courances,
Essonne, Ile-de-France

Foreword

In Greater Paris time weaves its tapestry of trees and flowers, pathways and fountains. A mantel of green splendor covers unsightliness; idyllic scenes mask scars from the past. Repulsion for a former wasteland transforms to revelry for a splendid landscaped scene. Richness of detail, precision of presentation and mastery of the overall production yield wondrous and complex works of art.

As with tapestry, park style often reflects the era of creation. A visit to parks around Paris means a trip through time as well as the many enjoyments of place. Built on the site of Roman baths in a place that has known settlement from the earliest times, the Cluny museum gardens in the St. Germain section of Paris reflect medieval uses, structure and design. Le Jardin des Plantes, le Jardin du Luxembourg and les Tuileries mirror the classical dignity of the Renaissance and the return to Greek and Roman ideals. André le Nôtre's formalistic, highly-stylized designs became the signature of landscaping in 17th-century France, imprinting virtually all the grand estates, especially those that encircled southern Paris. Although commissioned for private properties at the time, notable examples of his work – preserved to a greater or lesser extent – have opened for public visitation. Historic masterpieces such as Vaux le Vicomte, Sceaux, Versailles, St. Germain-en-Laye together compose the green fabric of Le Nôtre's legacy.

A discerning eye can find traces of multiple strands of development and change woven into certain parks. 17th-century Medici origins continue to be apparent in the palatial building style and long fountain leading to dramatic statuary, but also Emperor Napoléon III's 19th-century overlay, particularly in the pavilions and statuary. Other Napoleon III-era Haussmann projects like the Bois de Boulogne, the Parc Monceau and Champs-Elysées retain their 19th-century, English-inspired romantic airs.

Softer circular pathways replace angular rigidity; edifices play a supporting role to natural, but studied, randomness. Nature is presented in its asymmetric, though partially restrained, finery.

Medieval tapestry concepts such as allegory play a part in parks too. For example, the oak tree's symbolic reference to the renaissance and fertility associated with the coming of spring carries through to the 21st century. Pomegranate trees with their womb-shaped, seed-filled fruit evoke fecundity. Appealing to all the senses – taste, touch, sight, smell and hearing – remains a goal. The orange tree that blooms, produces fruit and is fragrant at the same time still claims a special place in the park. Sweet fragrances of fruit blossoms, the humming of bees and the feathery softness of the willow remain as iconic to garden lore as to tapestry topics. Threads such as these weave into today's garden sections devoted to scents, fruit trees, edible landscaping, vineyards and bee boxes, among others.

The integral element of parklands continues to be art. Art and nature interweave in unique and overarching ways in all parks. It follows, then, that artists have played a significant role throughout history in the preservation and development of open spaces. From medieval knot gardens to Rodin's sculpture gardens, artistic hands have shaped park design.

Amazing stories associate with the stunning heritage left by art communities of yore. »Pleine-air« painters took their canvas deep into the forests of Fontainebleau to show the world the reasons for preserving them. Although unknown to the untold numbers who enjoy the fruits of their labor today, the Barbizon artists' petitions and pictorial depictions resulted in the formation of the national forest at Fontainebleau. The fabled group that gathered in nearby Barbizon and other villages left an indelible mark of quaintness and charm, so that the villages themselves have become tributes to the artists' influences as well. Their reach spread in many ways and directions. After Claude Monet left Fontainebleau, he found the property in Giverny and created a wonderland of subject matter for his paintings that continues to attract an international following.

Thanks to Jules Gravereaux, a name recognized by very few, the whole world stops to smell roses around Paris. His artistry of intertwining roses in arcades, lattices, salons and arbors still can be appreciated in several roseraies. Portraitist Nélie Jacquemart left not only the images she painted of her husband but an entire abbey and its vast estate as museum and parklands. Famed sculptor Auguste Rodin gave France his two museums and his work to display in park and garden settings.

Like living tapestry, parks welcome the public to step into a world of natural wonder. Varied, plentiful and luxurious they set the stage for myriad scenes from renewal of spirit to scientific discovery. The greatest riches of Paris glow golden in fall, but grow green in the spring.

1. Square Louis XIII, Place des Vosges, 3rd arrondissement.

Scenes from a heavily wooded history

A long love of woodlands has been passed down through time to present inhabitants of Paris. In the days before notions of land-ownership took hold, roving tribes used rivers as roads and forests as storehouses. Well-stocked with berries and game, woods also supplied shelter and fuel for cooking, heating and forging metals.

Ancient reverence and hunting

Around the 3rd century BCE early European civilizations like La Tène and Hallstatt considered hilltops and lakes to be sacred. Oak groves drew Celtic Druid priests for rituals and ruling councils to meetings. The use of oak to smelt iron ore ushered in the Iron Age, further fueling the reverence for oaks generally and the ritual enshrinement of individual trees.

Historically populations have clustered around the Seine river's long narrow island now known as Ile de la Cité. Not only did the island afford protection from invasion, but the river was easier to ford there as well. From pre-Roman to Gallo-Roman times, the settlement of Lutetia claimed this area. Lutetia Parisiorum, Lukotekia, or in modern French, Lutèce are thought to be pre-Celtic terms for »marshlands«.

Evidence shows that about the 2nd century BCE, a tribe known as Parisii entered the area now known as Nanterre-Paris and based their main settlement around what is now the Ile de la Cité. At the time the densely wooded region offered good hunting grounds for bears, wolves, deer, otters and beavers. The Parisii stayed until the Roman era began, and along with the gold coins they left behind, they also gave Paris its current name.

Woods and gardens of the Roman Empire

Under Roman rule, the site along the Seine River achieved major importance within the province of Gallia Lugdunensis. By the time that the Romans controlled Paris in the 1st century BCE, their deities held divine sway over its land. From Julius Caesar's conquest of Lutetia through Rome's fall in the 5th century, the god Silvanus protected »uncultivated lands«. This pastoral deity was also charged with the guarding of flocks and herds.

For those defending against invaders, the woods served a practical purpose. When springtime brought hordes of storming Roman legions seizing humans and cattle, and burning houses and villages in their wake, the woods near Paris offered asylum to those fleeing the scourge. Roman armies harvested timber from European forests to construct their massive and numerous forts, but the thick woods could also impede movement of troops and hide local raiding parties. In the 5th century as the Roman Empire's dominance diminished, Germanic Frankish tribes gained ground. Cornerstones of Roman culture like the baths, markets and forums crumbled. The vibrancy of Greek and Roman literary and philosophical traditions declined in urban communities across the Continent.

About a century earlier in Ireland, the conservation of classical scholarship already had begun. Saint Patrick, a passionate supporter of books and proponent of green martyrdom, led the movement that revived and preserved western learning. Drawing on Egyptian aesthetic principles, he founded abbeys based on study, contemplation and a reverence for nature.

Manuscripts were collected and copied in abbeys that sprang up around Paris; gardens and vineyards became an integral part of abbey life. Contemplation and the appreciation for nature was harbored and fostered. Abbots and abbesses welcomed travelers and troubadours into their midst, stimulating communication as well as sharing literary traditions.

The Mérovingian dynasty that ruled France in the early Middle Ages donned the mantel of the Holy Roman Empire by taking over its organization. From the 5th through the 8th century the Mérovingians established their presence in multiple locations, particularly in what is now Paris and St. Denis. By the sword they commanded increasingly larger territories.

The Carolingian era commenced when Charlemagne was crowned in 800. »Charles the Great« promoted culture and education throughout the vast reaches of his expanding kingdom. Although illiterate himself, he nonetheless advocated education for both boys and girls.

Charlemagne's green decrees

At the time Charlemagne was crowned King of the Franks feudalism was gaining ever greater control of Europe. Rather than taking charge only in times of war according to common tribal custom, kings and princes started to keep their power and its trappings whether under siege or not. Individual ownership of property grew in popularity during this period.

Forests previously open to all became prized, elite possessions. Control of the trees meant wealth for the owner not only from the sale of timber, but from all the myriad benefits associated in and around the forests as well. Hunting grounds became a status symbol; an aristocrat's prominence was measured by the size of his woods.

In the 9th century Charlemagne issued capitularies in which he decreed the types of plants and fruit trees that were to be planted on royal estates in his realm. Examples among the various categories include

flowers: lilies and roses;

herbs: fenugreek, cumin, rosemary, burdock, caraway and fennel;

salads: cucumber, melon, rocket, parsley and lettuce;

potherbs: chicory, endive, beet and several kinds of mints;

roots: parsnip, carrot, onion, shallot, garlic;

fruit trees: apple, fig, pear, quince and mulberry;

nut trees: chestnut, hazel, almond and pine.

Gardens were carefully categorized in those days. The »hortus« section, as it was called in Latin, was reserved for growing vegetables. The »herbularius«, for medicinal herbs, needed to be small enough to reach the middle from all sides; pathways led to both sections, partially shaded

and furnished with benches. A third type of garden that began in the monasteries, »viridiarum«, was part orchard and part cemetery – essentially a graveyard among fruit trees. No single place was specially designated for flowers then, but they sprouted among the other plants and trees.

Emergence of medieval gardens

Charlemagne's empire marked a time of relative peace, so his numerous villas tended to be situated on flatlands. As enemy assaults increased following his reign, however, castles began to dominate the hilltops. For purposes of both defense and hunting, hilltops afforded the best vantage points and sites for fortresses.

As aristocratic strongholds grew in size, spaces inside the compounds began to be devoted to gardens. The larger the estate, the greater grew the parks and gardens. Most notably in Hesdin in northern France in 1288, at least 2000 acres belonged to the private park of Robert II of Artois, complete with fishponds, aviaries, menagerie, orchards, a rose garden, banquet pavilion, rolling hills and a marshy river. Plants ringed the fountains; benches graced the meadow. Herons, peacocks and swans ran free.

Other favorite medieval elements of parks and gardens included:

flowery meads, grassy benches, courtyards and moats,

palisades, vine-laced walls and trellises, gothic-style gateways,

woven grapevine fencing and borders,

canopied pathways, tunneled arcades, seat arbors, coppices,

launds, pollarded trees, willows,

outdoor rooms divided by walls and hedges,

orchards, vineyards protected against the foxes by thorn hedges,

medicinal plants, aromatic herbs, vegetables,

roses, forget-me-nots, hawthorns, columbines,

al-fresco tables for dining and toiling; banquet pavilion, springs, crenellated fountain,

linnets, blackbirds, nightingales, goldfinches, pheasants, partridges, doves, herons and peacocks to symbolize immortality,

hunting in the woods,

gathering in the garden,

fishing in the garden ponds.

The Middle Ages revitalized the ancient idea that rivers flowed from paradise. Water was esteemed in literature, tapestry and drawings as queen of all elements and the source of life. As with Roman predecessors, fountains played an important role in day-to-day life.

Beginning in the 12th century, a fourth type of garden grew popular with the ascendance of courtly love. The rose garden became the setting par excellence for romantic trysts, as depicted in writing and tapestry. Medieval parks created a world of fantasy for romantic encounters; enclosed gardens set the stage. The *Roman de la Rose*, the 13th-century allegorical poem that evolves around courtly love, began its tale in a walled garden and then moved to a park paradise.

For several centuries following the Middle Ages, parks and gardens appear to have remained almost exclusively in private estates.

Public parks from the 17th century

The Tuileries, the only park by landscape designer André Le Nôtre that was open to the public in the 17th century, signified a bold step that drew considerable consternation. In that period under King Louis XIV, many mansions with lavish formal gardens were designed by the famous trio of architect Louis Le Vau, artist Charles Le Brun and André Le Nôtre. Today several of those joint projects in the environs of Paris are open to the public; the Tuileries remains the only park by Le Nôtre within the city itself.

Previously as part of Catherine de Medici's gardens, the Tuileries already had been an open area near a palace that later burned down. Another Le Nôtre project in Paris is now occupied by the Parc de Bercy, but its prior use had encompassed an older park belonging to the old Bercy castle which was destroyed in 1861. Yet another prior land use in the Parc de Bercy location was that of wine warehouse district with rails connecting it to the quais along the Seine.

Versailles, Vaux le Vicomte, St. Germain-en-Laye, Saint-Cloud, Sceaux, Fontainebleau, and Chantilly, though designed as private gardens by Le Nôtre at the time, have now all been opened for public use. Lying within reach of the city, all count among favorite destinations for Parisians.

A green treasury from the Second Empire

The signature grand green spaces of Paris derive from Napoleon III's plan to improve Parisian life. Planted roadways radiating from circles – known as stars or étoiles – and the grand, wide, tree-lined drives of Avenues Foch and Georges Mandel remain as archetypal elements of the style from the era of Napoleon III.

Napoleon III had returned from his exile in England, inspired by London's parks that were treasured by both rich and poor. His Préfet of the Seine Baron Haussmann carried out orders to clean up and beautify Paris, creating parklands and giving rise to the elegant buildings, boulevards and urban design that are usually associated with Haussmann's name. Under the direction of Baron Haussmann and engineer Jean-Charles Alphand, 600,000 trees and 180,000 acres of forest and gardens were added to the French realm. Within the space of 17 years the city was cloaked in an elegant verdant mantel, open to all. Le Bois de Boulogne, le Bois de Vincennes, les Buttes-Chaumont, le Parc Monceau, le Jardin de Luxembourg, the Squares, l'Avenue de l'Impératrice (now Avenue Foch), les Jardins des Champs-Elysées, les Jardins du Trocadéro, les Plantations d'Alignement and les Promenades sur les Boulevards plantés number among the greatest accomplishments from that period.

The impact of wide tree-lined boulevards on the look and feel of Paris cannot be underestimated. In a deviation from Napoleon III's vision for the city, architect Charles Garnier insisted that no trees be allowed to obstruct the view of his landmark opera building. When compared with the boulevards from the same era that are graced by rows of towering trees, Avenue de l'Opéra appears stark, unprotected by nature's sentinels and unsoftened by foliage.

2. Milly-la-Forêt, Essonne. Medieval-style garden feature: wisteria-shaded pathway.
3. Château de Courances, Essonne, Ile-de-France.

While Paris was undergoing its transformation, Napoleon III granted the plea of a band of artists in a forest further south. Fontainebleau became one of the world's first national forests.

A 19th-century artist colony at Barbizon and the campaign for Fontainebleau

Art and nature have always maintained a special relationship, but the successes of Fontainebleau yielded lasting triumphs for both. The artists who gathered at Barbizon ended up ushering in the new era of Impressionism while preserving majestic rocks and forestlands.

The tale begins in 1830 when Camille Corot moved to the small village of Barbizon in order to paint light filtering through the nearby forests of Fontainebleau. Soon painters Théodore Rousseau, Diaz de la Pena, Félix Ziem, Constant Troyon and Jean-François Millet followed him and together they formed the Barbizon School. Paul Cézanne and Paul Emile Pissarro joined them a few years later, and Claude Monet later still.

Increasingly alarmed about the destruction of the forests, Corot issued his clarion call on canvas. He used his paintings to show the urgent need for preservation. The artists' efforts also caught the attention of photographers and conservationists.

In 1852 Théodore Rousseau made a direct appeal to Napoleon III, who answered the petition by decreeing part of the forest to be a nature preserve in 1853. This in itself would be a stunning achievement for the group of plein-air artists whose outdoor studios still ignite the imagination of romantics today. As yet another outgrowth of the plein-air movement, Claude Monet created his gardens at Giverny.

Giverny's emergence as an art and garden scene

By 1859 Camille Corot's work in Fontainebleau had captured the attention of 19-year-old Claude Monet at a salon exhibit featuring three of the Barbizon painters. Four years later Monet stayed at a village close enough to Barbizon to observe the painting group firsthand. Meanwhile he also had become acquainted with the work of Gustave Courbet, Auguste Renoir, Alfred Sisley, Paul Emile Pissarro and Paul Cézanne.

Sometime later Monet looked out of the window of a train he was riding and instantly chose the charming little spot called Giverny to be his own artistic headquarters. Despite being a place of considerable historic significance, with ruins from Gallo-Roman, Mérovingian and medieval habitation, Giverny had managed to maintain its small-town charm. In 1880 Monet bought a house and enough land to begin his famous gardens.

Almost a century later yet another strand of art history wove its way into Giverny. In 1992 Chicagoan Daniel Terra's foundation opened the Musée d'Art Américain in Giverny, complete with extensive gardens. Today Giverny remains an oasis of Impressionist art, welcoming global visitors to both the Monet house and gardens and the Musée des Impressionnismes in Giverny.

Rodin's studios and museums

Auguste Rodin's talents, foresight and planning have given the public not only his world-famous work, but also two museums in which to display it. The gardens at both locations serve as settings for his monumental sculptures, both with intimate outdoor salons and expansive green galleries.

Following the green city's grand tradition

Park projects swell Parisian green coffers with new spaces, conversions of industrial areas and lining streets with trees. The promotion of natural arts, sciences, sustainability and innovation acts to insure and expand sound environmental practices. The number of Paris parks, gardens and squares distributed throughout the city far exceeds four hundred and continues to grow in number.

The city regularly exhibits the intricacies of park development, construction and maintenance, and offers related career opportunities. On website *www.paris.fr* the mayor's office posts an English version of current information on parks and gardens, including the frequent and instructive »Fêtes des Jardins« held at the parks. These fully staffed events present complementary opportunities for sophisticated learning about up-to-the-minute ecological practices.

Vague traces of antiquity

When strolling through the parks one is enveloped by nature's beauty, but also beguiled by historical and artistic references. In the pages to come the reader is invited to take a chronological tour of some of the vicinities that have played a vital role in bestowing the Ile de France with its hallowed green allure.

Commencing with the Romans

Although no ruins have survived from Roman times to further grace the Square du Vert-Galant, still the hideaway framed by the Seine on both sides seems a fitting place for beginnings. Roman devotion to water – thermal springs, aqueducts or artisian wells – seems to be memorialized in this diminutive mid-river retreat.

At the site of probably the first human occupation of the Paris area, one cannot help but sense the importance of the Seine to all habitants from antiquity onwards. The variety of vegetation and the elegant simplicity of design well reflect the superior crafting and use of public open space generally in the Paris environs.

Another place of ancient Roman activity that deserves note, the restored sports arena and coliseum of the Arènes du Lutèce, lies a short distance south of the Seine. About midway between Vert-Galant and Arènes de Lutèce, the Cluny museum and gardens occupy the thermal baths used by the Romans some two thousand years ago. Archaeological excavations of the ruins can be viewed inside the museum.

Jumping ahead in time, the history of the Gobelin tapestry museum and current Square

René Le Gall developed along a river, although it is now-subterranean. Dye and weaving production thrived at this site, and later became the royal manufactory with extensive gardens.

Square du Vert-Galant, 1st arrondissement

Inherently a romantic yet practical location, the wedge of land now known as Ile de la Cité surfaces midway in the Seine. Water still flows on both sides of the slender point known as Vert-Galant. A stairway slips down to it unobtrusively from the heavily traveled bridge road.

Hidden in plain view, the dew-drop shaped park crouches low, its green serenity sequestering it from the crowds. The city radiates around the tip that is reputed to be Paris' oldest settlement. Viewed from across the river, however, the park looks like the grounds of a grand estate with no visible entrance.

Early on, this part of the island contained a Mérovingian palace. Home to »long-haired kings« Merovech, Childeric, Clovis, Clotaire, Dagobert and Chilperic, this dynasty began its rule of the area known as Francia in the middle of the 5th century. Starting with the part called »Neutria« on the western shore, the Salian Franks kings conquered most of present-day France and Germany. By dividing plunder only among their inner circle, they advanced feudalistic practices on the European Continent.

In the 18th century, harking back to Roman tradition, commercial baths operated in this location and were shielded by rows of trees. Today's park contains maple, apple, Bohemian olive, catalpa, robinier and gingko trees.

Les Arènes de Lutèce, 5th arrondissement

The original Roman amphitheater occupied this site from the 1st to the 3rd century CE it was not until the late 19th and into the early 20th century that the land was acquired and the modified reconstruction completed. In the intervening time, a street named the Rue Monge had been cut through the site, foreclosing the possibility of a true replication. The arena held 17,000 spectators.

Hôtel de Cluny, 5th arrondissement

It stands to reason that some of the oldest ruins in Paris can be found close to the Ile de la Cité. Situated as it is in the middle of the Seine, the island has drawn settlements from time immemorial due to the relative easy of crossing the river there. Just a short distance to the south of the Ile lies a great treasure trove of Parisian history.

Vestiges of Roman influence can be seen other places in the city too, but the ruins under the Cluny museum suggest the central role this site played in Roman life in terms of water. Excavation of thermal baths can be partially seen from the street, and to a greater extent inside the museum. As a critical part of everyday living, the baths no doubt enjoyed a prime location in the early Roman settlement.

To most people »Cluny« usually calls up the magnificent Gothic mansion in St. Germain. The Romanesque Cluny abbey founded in 910 in Bourgogne near Mâcon held the position of wealthiest, most powerful institution of its kind in Europe in that era. The left bank Cluny simply acted as the Paris residence for the abbots of the main one.

In the 14th century the abbots directed that their new Paris residence be built on the ruins of the 2nd- and the 3rd-century Roman Lutetia's thermal baths. In its prime, the reach of the abbey at Cluny included the British Isles and was second only in size to St. Peter's Basilica in Rome. Now one-tenth that size, the main abbey at Cluny houses the national school of arts and crafts. In the first half of the 19th century the Paris Cluny became a museum.

The deep reaches of the Cluny yield ancient history, but the top floor guards its own treasury of crafted riches. The six parts of *The Lady and the Unicorn* tapestry contain a wealth of historical references not only to the era in which they were woven, but also to ancient history. Five are devoted to the senses and one to »mon seul désir«.

At first glance the scenes portrayed in the monumental weavings might seem completely idyllic and fanciful. It is hard to imagine that lions and one-horned hoofed creatures would have roamed ancient Lutetia. A look at the broader picture, however, gives the idea of the enormous stock given by antiquity to nature's allure.

Placing activities outdoors among trees and flowers glorifies even the most common acts, whether playing an instrument, looking in the mirror or savoring delicacies. This formula remains the common denominator for every tapestry in the set: trees framing the activity and flowers throughout. Figures wearing finest brocades engage in pageantry, further emphasizing the grandeur of nature.

Appreciating the magnificent medieval weavings can enhance the appreciation of the medieval gardens outside. The garden is divided into four parts: the kitchen garden, the herb garden, the symbolic garden and the rose garden which represents the ideals of courtly love. Placards indicate the types of trees and their allegorical significance. Because of the lack of archeological evidence, and because no medieval gardens have survived in their original form, scholars have derived notions of the very early medieval garden primarily from illuminated manuscripts and written references.

After Rome fell in the 5th century, gardens are generally thought to have moved inside abbey and castle walls because of the uncertainty of the times. Gardens for both medicinal and alimentary purposes necessarily shrunk in size during the early Middle Ages due to the more confined spaces. The scale of the medieval garden at the Cluny may thus be generally representative of size as well as content from those times.

Gothic tapestry chronicles

The fine art of tapestry commands a place of honor in the annals of art and garden lore.

Woven scenes provide a view into a period whose art tends otherwise to be devoted to religious themes. Medieval tapestry hung on expansive castle walls; stained glass windows claimed soaring cathedral spaces. Woven subject matter thus tended toward secular themes.

Although the flora may not have always been portrayed with rigid exactitude – like pomegranates growing on frond-leaved trees, for example – still the overall settings and effects give an idea of the customs and manners considered important enough to be memorialized at the time. Treasured and chosen as gifts of state, tapestry attained revered status in the 15th century, especially by the powerful Dukes of Burgundy.

Artists who designed cartoons, the full-sized patterns placed behind the warp threads, typically lived at the court and were treated with high regard. Looms were set up on site and pieces were created specifically for particular walls.

Tapestry production calls Flanders to mind, but many workshops thrived in France earlier on. The town of Arras, known for tapestry woven of gold and silk threads in 14th- and 15th-century France, serves as an example. By the 16th century weavers had moved their operations to Flanders.

The gobelin tapestry manufactory and the Square René Le Gall, 13th arrondissement

Beneath the René Le Gall gardens flows a stream that played an integral part in the enterprise that made this sector famous. In the 15th century a family named Gobelin began their dyeing business on the banks of the Bièvre. Only in 1938 when the square opened to the public was the water channellized underground.

By the 16th century the Gobelin dyeing business had developed into an uncommonly successful tapestry workshop. In 1662 the government under Louis XIV bought the tapestry operation and combined it with the royal furniture manufactory. Although the manufactory continues to produce monumental, hand-woven tapestry and teach traditional techniques, the primary building has become a museum with rotating exhibits of weaving masterpieces.

René Le Gall occupies much of the area that had been kitchen gardens for the artisans working for the Gobelin manufactory. In part its design recalls those 15th- and 16th-century times, while the gloriettes, or gazebos, add a romantic touch.

Like the Cluny museum's mille-fleurs tapestry, the woven flora and fauna of the Gobelin tapestry collection contain numerous allegorical references. Roman-style figures wearing togas suggest everyday activities. One scene shows an outdoor court under a canopy of grapevines in which an accused is being brought to justice. In another, cupids with watering cans tend a flowerbed.

Early public medicinal gardens, the heritage of herbal cures

Given the importance of medicinal herbs throughout history, they must have appeared in the gardens of those who made the first transplants of edible vegetation, those who realized the advantage of growing plants in one place rather than gathering them from near and far. Pliny the Elder discussed the medicinal benefits of plants in first century Rome; garlic, yarrow, marigold and tarragon were likely administered to Roman soldiers. Charlemagne took such an interest in natural herbs that he mandated certain ones to be planted by the subjects in the 9th-century Holy Roman Empire.

Carrying forward the long tradition of natural medicine, the Jardin des Plantes deserves particular recognition for its early efforts to establish a public medicinal garden that continues to follow its original charter of natural science.

Jardin des Plantes, 5th arrondissement

For close to four centuries this park has been devoted to science. Even today the gardens carry forward a distinctively didactic purpose, with informational placards of graphics and detailed descriptions. Alpine, ecological, botanical, zoological gardens as well as horticulture, paleontology, mineralogy and evolution exhibits provide edification whatever the weather.

In 1640 a medicinal herb garden about one quarter the size of today's Jardin des Plantes opened to the public. Initiated by physicians to Louis XIII as a source of medication for those in need, it was also used for research by the medical school. By the end of the 17th century, botanical and zoological gardens and an amphitheater for teaching chemistry had been added, and it had become a center for the era's most distinguished scientists.

The Grand Galerie with its gracious allées, roseraie, labyrinthe, rotonde and amphitheater adds immeasurable charm. The ancient tree of Judah, the Indian chestnut and the cedar of Lebanon all date back to the 18th century; the park houses 400 types of irises and 800 animals. The romance of the park's design draws artists, some of whom are commissioned by the park to prepare materials and books.

In addition to the vast array of longstanding scientific interest, the park continues to be well known for its aesthetics. The conservatory stands out as a 19th-century innovation in the use of glass and iron. In a tradition that carries through to the present, design features have been carefully crafted, from signposts to drain covers.

Palatial settings

The Le Nôtre heritage; André Le Nôtre and 17th-century design (1613–1700)

Growing up quite literally in the Tuileries gardens, André Le Nôtre learned skills from his gardener father and eventually followed him into the position of head gardener. Living next door to the Palais du Louvre also served him well, since at the time part of the Louvre contained the academy of the arts. There he studied classical art and perspective, mathematics, painting and architecture.

In 1657 Le Nôtre began his first major project at Château de Vaux le Vicomte for Nicolas Fouquet, Louis XIV's head of finances. In 1661 he worked for the king himself to enhance the garden and parks at the Château de Versailles. For the town of Versailles he designed the grand Avenue de Paris, still a primary feature.

Fontainebleau, Saint-German en Laye, Saint-Cloud, Chantilly, the Champs-Elysées, Sceaux and Marly counted among his projects. He also provided designs for London's Greenwich Park, remodeled gardens near Turin, Italy, and sent advice on a project to Germany. A number of his projects that still exist lie within easy reach of Paris and are now open to the public.

Antiquity inspired 17th-century landscape designers with notions of clipped trees, canals, labyrinths and crystal palaces. Other popular ideas were that diversity embellishes gardens and that the garden needed to be positioned with regard to the lay of the land. The form of gardens, the allées and promenades, parterres, relief, water enhancements, running rivers and brooks, fountains, canals to carry water to the fountains, grottoes, aviaries, espaliers and pleasure gardens all played prominently in garden design of that era.

Lakes were considered the eyes of the ocean, springs the upwelling of the seas. Basic fundamentals for design held that

art should give way to nature,
gardens should keep from looking gloomy,
gardens should not disclose too much, and
gardens should appear larger than they
really are.

Designs always should be grand and beautiful.
Oblong gardens seem more graceful.

To reach the garden, one should descend at least three steps from a building. The parterre needs to be seen first, closest to the building and kept small relative to the rest.

Woods and bosquets give relief to a garden. Elevated places add grace, marking and partitioning off spaces. Woods should be near a parterre, but never a lawn by a basin. Avoid void on void; rather place a solid against a void and the flat against relief. Geometric topiary adds interest.

The opening of the Tuileries gardens for public use was a source of much discussion. As the 17th-century head of royal buildings, Jean-Baptiste Colbert feared damage. To the argument of poet Charles Perrault that »it would be a public affliction not to be able to come here to walk about«, Colbert responded: »It is only idlers who come here.« Whereupon Perrault replied: »People come here ... to take the air; they come here to talk about business, about marriages, and about everything which is dealt with more appropriately in a garden. ...«

The public gained access.

Jardin des Tuileries, 1st arrondissement

»Tile works« doesn't carry the same élan, but in the 12th century the term would have been descriptive of the Tuileries district. Then the view along the Seine that is now graced by the Louvre's expansive gardens would have been quite different. »Tuile« means »tile« and »tuileries« the noisy, dusty manufactories where tiles were crafted.

The tilemakers had taken over an area previously occupied by vineyards, pasturelands, and fields, with a few living shelters scattered through it. Catherine de Médici brought the first castle – the old Louvre – and its lavish gardens into being around 1564. The biggest contributor to its present look, however, was 17th-century landscape designer André Le Nôtre.

On the »axe historique«, one of the most-heavily traveled walkways in the world, the Louvre is linked with the Champs-Elysées by way of the Place de la Concorde. In Paris the Tuileries gardens remain as the sole example of Le Nôtre's work that most closely approximates his original design.

A number of his other gardens featured in this book have been chosen because of their historical importance, present day significance, intrinsic value, singularity, esteem by Parisians and ease of access. André Le Nôtre developed some 50 landscaping plans for country mansions during this same period, a good many of which are located near Fontainebleau.

The original formality envisioned by André Le Nôtre in his plans for the Tuileries gardens can be seen in the way the trees are trimmed, the angularity of the spaces he defined, the Greek and Roman-inspired sculptures, and the golden touches in the grillwork. As an example, a marble Pericles is shown bestowing crowns to the artists. The 5th century BCE Athenian was known for fostering literature and the arts as well as democracy. Although placed in the garden in 1835, a century after Le Nôtre's time, the statue follows the neoclassical theme.

Behind Pericles stands a white mulberry tree. In antiquity mulberry trees grew near temples for dual purposes. The berries fed the faithful as well as the worms that produced highly prized silks.

Statues of a more contemporary nature carry forward the classical tradition of combining sculpture and garden. Along the grand promenade, towering figures on pedestals prepare the way for monuments ahead. Some smaller segments off the main trunk create intimate areas, combining art, form and dining.

Château de Courances, Essonne

The origins of the exquisite park at Courances have elicited considerable discussion. The administrative plan of Courances dates back at least to a 1627 survey; André Le Nôtre was born in 1613. Although timing precludes him from authorship of the park, records from the era show that his father Jean, head gardener of the Tuileries, was involved early on. He was most probably a part of an initial phase of expansion.

The acquisition of small manors and other lands effectively linked the château with the village. In this aspect of the property development André Le Nôtre most probably played a significant role. It is likely that his influence is felt in the estate as a whole because of his late-stage involvement.

Château de Fontainebleau, Seine-et-Marne

In the mid-12th century, Fontainebleau served as a hunting lodge and chapel for Louis VII. In the 13th century the great patron of the arts Louis IX, or »Saint Louis«, cherished it as his wilderness and also added a country house and hospital.

Although the design of the estate has been changed many times throughout its history, one of the oldest artifacts remains in the garden. Dating from 1603, the statue of Roman goddess Diane the huntress adorns a fountain, surrounded by her four bronze dogs. Functionally, the carp pond harkens back to medieval concept of dedicating part of the garden to raising fish for household consumption.

Already in 1543 Fontainebleau had gained recognition for its grotto of the pines, the first such edifice known in France. In 1601 white mulberry trees were planted and buildings constructed at Fontainebleau and the Tuileries for the breeding of silkworms. In the first half of the 17th century the Pavé de Roy road led from Paris to Fontainebleau, easing the transportation between the two favored places.

From 1645/46 André Le Nôtre worked on plans and execution of the gardens at Fontainebleau. Although altered considerably from their original scheme, his style can still be detected. Garden-related enterprises flourished, including a mole-catching service that boasted having caught 2723 of them in Fontainebleau, Versailles and St. Germain.

Fontainebleau – changed from »fontaine belle eau« to its current name in 1169 – lies just about 50 kilometers southeast of Paris.

Château de St. Germain-en-Laye, Yvelines

Perched on the plateau with a sweeping view of the river valley that wraps around it, St. Germain-en-Laye has attracted coteries to establish their residences in this quiet, convenient location just to the west of Paris. André Le Nôtre capitalized on the expansive views with his design of a mile-and-a-half-long terrace; his plans also encompassed the park and forest. Five and a half million trees were planted on the estate in 1665.

Vineyards overlooking the river evoke the ones that grew there in the 8th century. In 2000 the agricultural and horticultural school revived the tradition by planting 1900 vines of Pinot noir according to André Le Nôtre's original scheme. Elaborate waterworks in the castle's grottoes served as precursors to the massive projects undertaken at Versailles by the same family of Italian engineers.

Cultural events staged here drew poets and writers including the master of comic theater Jean-Baptiste Poquelin, known as Molière (1622 to 1673). In the 19th-century hotel that opened in the Pavillon Henri IV, writers, artists and politicians gathered regularly. Alexandre Dumas composed two novels while staying here. Within the town itself, the home of famed music composer Claude Debussy is open to the public.

Collections contained in the museum of national antiquities here evidence habitation back to the Paleolithic Stone Age, some million years ago. Artifacts from various other ages like La Tène, Gallo-Roman and Mérovingian are also on display.

Château de Vaux le Vicomte, Seine et Marne

Reflective pools, grand canal, channels, grottoes and moat set the splendor of what is arguably André Le Nôtre's landscaping masterpiece. Even more spectacular than the grounds, however, is the rise and demise of the one who commissioned the work, Nicolas Fouquet. Viewed as a young genius, Fouquet had held a position in par-

liament at age 20, then procurer general, then superintendent of finances.

In creating an estate worthy of his elevated status, Fouquet gathered the leading lights of the day: architect Louis Le Vau, artist Charles Le Brun and landscape designer André Le Nôtre. Three villages were demolished to make way for his grand plans. Twelve hundred fountains and cascades were installed.

Charles Le Brun set up a tapestry workshop nearby to meet the mansion's specifications. Later the workshop moved to Paris and became the royal Gobelin manufactory, charged with producing palatial furniture. As head of both the industrial arts through the Gobelin and the entire art world through the academy, Le Brun left an indelible imprint on all art of the period.

A fateful day in 1661 stopped short Fouquet's lavishness. In an extravaganza in which Molière himself acted in a new play against a lush backdrop of greenery, Fouquet drew the ire of Louis XIV for outdoing him. Less than three weeks later Fouquet was arrested for having mixed his own finances with the king's.

Louis Le Vau, Charles Le Brun and André Le Nôtre met with a quick shift of task. They were enlisted to create the palace and gardens at Versailles. Fouquet remained imprisoned for life, abandoned by his former entourage except for fabulist La Fontaine and letter-writer par excellence Marie de Rabutin-Chantal, known as Mme. de Sévigné.

Much of André Le Nôtre's grand design remains intact here, most notable the baroque axis that reaches out to infinity. Although privately owned, Vaux le Vicomte is designated as a historic monument and is open to the public.

Château de Versailles, Yvelines

Beginning in 1661 André Le Nôtre worked to extend the hunting grounds and lodging for Louis XIV as well as to lay out the entire town of Versailles which today retains to a large extent its original basic design. Although altered many times through the years, the gardens still hold intact some aspects of Le Nôtre's 17th-century planning. Before the installation of the gardens, however, came the massive water projects reminiscent of ancient Roman undertakings.

The development at Versailles employed the use of preassembled iron pipes and recycled water supplies. A double-circuit system separated drinking water from the hydraulic installations that fed 1400 water jets. Techniques of design and organization of the Versailles gardens came to be applied in urban planning as well: the central axis, star-pointed intersections, attention to perspective.

Château de Sceaux, Hauts-de-Seine

First written mention of Sceaux comes from the 12th century when a group of parishioners broke away from the earlier-established Châtenay to commence their own congregation. In the 17th century Colbert, heir to the property now occupied by the castle, aggrandized the estate. In compensation for the lands he took, he built the first two public fountains for the village; until then there had been only wells and cisterns.

Colbert, controller general to Louis XIV, at first protested the lavish spending of Fouquet in Vaux, and then even that of his own king in Versailles. Sceaux, however, turned out to be perfectly situated, close to Paris and on the way from the king's Fontainebleau residence to Versailles. Soon he built himself a magnificent estate on his vast holdings. Like Fontainebleau, in Sceaux a significant project of canalization was undertaken and the unusual incline of the property lent itself to the creation of elaborate cascades. André Le Nôtre placed the castle at the crossing of the two axes of the landscape design, giving a sweeping view of the entire length of the channels down to the horizon. Adhering to 17th-century English philosopher Frances Bacon's maxim, Le Nôtre obeyed nature in order to command it.

In 1846 the arrival of the railroad connected Sceaux with Paris, greatly increasing its popularity. Even today Sceaux remains well connected. The RER from Paris splits just to the north; one branch stops at the Parc du Sceaux and the other near the main pedestrian shopping street.

Château de Saint-Cloud, Hauts-de-Seine

A nature preserve until 1923, the park and gardens overlooking the Seine here are considered among the most beautiful in Europe and finest among Le Nôtre's designs. Associated with a former palace and destroyed in the late 19th century, the palace had been occupied by Florentine bankers associated with the Medici family in the 16th century. Originally the garden was designed in an Italianate style with a series of landscaped terraces stepping down the hill and fountains at each level.

André Le Nôtre created the Grand Cascade, the centerpiece of the current plan, as well as the gardens à la française. Marie Antoinette's rose garden continues to be used by for state purposes. A viewpoint known as »La Laterne« stems from the days when an illuminated lantern at that site signaled the presence of Napoleon I.

Château de Meudon, Hauts-de-Seine

Views from the terraces designed by André Le Nôtre memorialize his deftness with terracing. From the long cool allées running high along the valley's walls, the vistas of the Seine and the Eiffel Tower still lend entrancing views. The style of the era can still be seen in the façade of the Orangerie and the Observatoire, flanked by spectacular trees and woods.

Château de Chantilly, Oise

Housing one of the finest art galleries in France, Chantilly castle has been owned primarily by the Montmorency family since the 16th century. Upon the death of the previous owner Henri d'Orléans, Duc d'Aumale, the property passed to the Institut de France in 1897.

Best known for its grand horse stables and hippodrome, Chantilly contains a period-piece performance ring. Molière's play *Les Précieuses Ridicules* debuted here in 1659. According to author Madame de Sévigné, famous for her letters that revealed glimpses of courtly life, the maitre d'hôtel to the Grand Condé took his own life at the possibility that the fish course would not be served on time.

Premiere royal Parisian squares

The following two examples of 17th-century style lend classical elegance to the areas that surround them. Both feature graceful arcades that run the entire length of the buildings enclosing the squares; both feel like jewel boxes with their bright floral arrays. Entering through passageways from busy streets, a visitor finds an immediate calm. In terms of the difference in pace, these spaces seem to be microcosms of country life held deep within the city while maintaining a superb urban sophistication.

Palais Royal, 1st arrondissement

Despite the wide-ranging affairs that may or may not have taken occurred here in the past four centuries, the Palais Royal retains its regal bearing. In Paris its gardens keep the reputation of premiere meeting place. Its fountains, deep shaded allées and statuary make easy landmarks; its arcaded perimeter offers strolling, refreshment and shopping.

Cardinal Richelieu commissioned the original palace in the early part of the 17th century, and for a time it was known as »Palais Cardinal«. As »chief minister« or »first minister« to Louis XIII, Cardinal Richelieu is reputed to have believed that the end justifies the means, and that he could take six lines from the most honest person and hang him with them. Some revere him as France's greatest politician.

Later in the 17th century, parts of the ruling family from the house of Orléans occupied the premises, using the building either as primary or ancillary quarters.

In the 18th century the Duke of Orléans Louis Philippe Joseph d'Orléans, or Philippe Egalité as he became known, offered the Palais Royal as refuge to Jacobins who were spreading the egalitarian philosophy of Jean-Jacques Rousseau and Montesquieu in the French Revolution. An Anglophile, Philippe made many trips to Great Britain in the late 1700s and embraced ideas of the Enlightenment. He opened the Palais Royal gardens to the general public for the first time, and also allowed shops to locate in the arcades.

In 1799 the Comédie Française located to the Palais Royal and still continues to perform at this location. Other occupants include the Constitutional Council and the Ministry of Culture, whose offices are housed in the wings of the building added in the early 19th century. The architect of the original façades, Victor Louis, had also designed Bordeaux' Grand Théâtre.

Square Louis XIII, Place des Vosges, 3rd arrondissement

186 linden trees have adorned the square since 1976, although other roots reach much further back into history. The square's appearance in the 1600s under Henry IV drew superlatives as one of the sweetest blossoms of classical architecture, graced with its 37 pavilions. Since 1840 four signature fountains, symmetrically placed, have defined the space within Paris' oldest planned square.

Two other past dwellers of the regal residences ringing the green are revered in French literature: Victor Hugo and Madame de Sévigné. A museum commemorates the home of the 19th-century author of *Les Misérables*.

The Napoleon III legacy

A Transformative turn of fate

19th-century Parisian history spins a tale of Heraclean-scale makeovers against all odds – from the deplorable to the magnificent, unspeakable to sensational. Without a bold turn of fate in the mid-1800s, the city easily could have remained the gargantuan set for a horror story. Its forestlands had been torn and burned by endless wars, its terrain blighted by corpse-filled caverns.

If time's curtain could be pulled back to show the scene in Paris in the early 1800s, it would shock all the senses. The lack of sanitation would have played a huge part in the olfactory onslaught, as well as the visual. Odious as that may have been, it was far from the worst of it.

At this point it is important to remember that the area Paris now claims had been inhabited over millennia, and the remains of many habitants had been duly inhumed. The numbers over those years began to accumulate into the millions. The decision was made to move all human remains out of the city.

One more piece of information bears mentioning here. The area just to the south of the city, as it then existed, had supplied stone for massive building projects up until that time. The huge quarrying ventures left immense pits, tunnels and underground channels. It was to these vast wastelands that the centuries-long buildup of mankind's detritus was carried – by carriage by dark of night.

Bois de Boulogne, 16th arrondissement

Napoleon III instructed Haussmann to beautify Paris, to bring the best of the rest of the world into the city for Parisians to enjoy at their convenience. The distribution of open spaces was to be even, with parklands of various sizes easily reachable in all areas. This section looks at the four anchor parks, north, south, east and west, and a sampling of others.

The Bois de Boulogne and the Bois de Vincennes already existed as hunting grounds associated with royal residences, but each had suffered from past wars and misuse. Parc des Buttes-Chaumont and Parc Montsouris, replacing

what likely had been the most despicable dumping grounds for waste of every imaginable description, called for extensive engineering and terrain modification. According to some accounts of the triumphal opening of such a transformation at Parc Montsouris, the water suddenly disappeared from the lake, to the terminal consternation of the official in charge.

Across a planted bridgeway bordering the west edge of Paris stretches the bountiful Bois de Boulogne. A mere vestige of its former size, the ancient Bois de Rouvray from the Roman days of Lutèce spread all the way to Compiègne. Referenced for the first time in the Charter of Compiègne in 717, the name Rouvray derives from the red oak, quercus robur, the characteristic tree of the forest. For the kings of France the forests long served as an exhibit of their wealth and grounds for entertaining heads of state.

Wars wreaked havok on the Rouvray woodlands. Immense quantities of timber were removed to build ships and castles. Politics chopped the land into many pieces.

Napoleon Bonaparte took steps to reforest, but with the return of war in 1814 and 1815, the trees suffered once again. In 1848 the forests became the property of the state, and in 1852 owned by the city of Paris. Napoleon III took a personal interest in the development of the Bois de Boulogne, directing that it be modeled after English parks.

The stream running through the Bois de Boulogne probably owes its existence to the time that Napoleon III spent in London. Inspired by Hyde Park and the stream running through it, the ruler set about to provide something similar in Paris in 1852. The water meandered its way through cascades and caves fashioned of rocks brought from Fontainebleau, the royal residence south of Paris.

The Pré-Catelan and Jardin Shakespeare in the Bois de Boulogne feature vegetation chosen as proper illustration for five of Shakespeare's poems. The 400-seat theater in the green offers both classical and modern performances in the season.

Under Napoleon III 420,000 trees were planted. 66 kilometers of subterranean conduits for water were laid; 24 pavilions were built. Kiosques, embarcaderos, caves, balustrades were added as embellishments. Excavations from the creation of two lakes were used to form Butte Montmartre.

Paths wind their way along 35 kilometers of the park. Bike and riding trails combined add another 37 kilometers. Only the Reine Marguerite and Longchamp allées were laid out in a straight line.

The Bagatelle – »bauble« or »trinket« – castle reputedly was constructed in 67 days on a bet with Queen Marie-Antoinette. The brother of Louis XIV, Comte d'Artois, won the bet in 1777, after employing a legion of workers at great expense. Even before its extensive renovation in the comte's hands, it had been a longtime favorite gathering spot for lavish parties and hunting expeditions. Today the Bagatelle contains one of the most beautiful rose gardens – roseraies – in Paris.

The Chalet des Iles, created in 1854 on the biggest of the forest's two isles, claims its origin as an authentic Swiss chalet. It was carried in sepa-

7. Portrait of Emperor Napoléon III. From: Anne Dion-Tenenbaum, *The Napoléon III Apartments*, Musée du Louvre Editions, Paris, 2006, frontispiece.

rate pieces from Switzerland to the isle. The café-restaurant, which doubles as a theater with ballroom and concert hall, came into being at the end of the 19th century.

The Jardin d'Acclimatation, inaugurated by Napoléon III in 1860, offers exhibits and activities for the young, including a marionette show and museums of flora and fauna. A small train runs to the Jardin from the Porte Maillot. Rowing, bicycling and horseback riding remain favorite forms of recreation in the park.

The Emperor's Kiosque stands as tribute to Napoleon III who is primarily responsible for the way the Bois de Boulogne looks today.

Bois de Vincennes, 12th arrondissement

The first mention of the forest of Vilcena appeared in document from 847. By the 12th century Philippe Auguste burned part of the thick woods to facilitate the hunt. Legend has it that in the 13th century Saint Louis dispensed justice under an oak in the Vincennes forest. In the 18th century under Louis XV Vincennes was opened to the public, although it even now remains a preserve for hunting.

Under Napoleon III Haussmann created three lakes, implemented an English-style park and turned the formerly straight roads into more curving ones. To balance the east and west edges of Paris, Napoleon III and his team wanted the amenities in the Bois de Vincennes to be similar. Hence the features of Vincennes were modeled after those of the Bois de Boulogne. However, the costs and difficulties involved with the formation of the Bois de Vincennes ran considerably higher. Prior land uses as industrial sites and lack of available water created bigger challenges with more expensive solutions.

Today the park contains 100 kilometers of walking paths, 23 kilometers of bicycling trails and 19 kilometers of horse trails. Four lakes, an arboretum, a farm, a hippodrome, a velodrome, a tropical garden and Parc Floral add to the park's allure.

Parc des Buttes-Chaumont, 10th arrondissement

The quarry dated back to Roman times, and the Montaucon gibbet conducted its public executions here in the Middle Ages. Brigands and thieves hid in the old abandoned quarry grounds, and a battle against the Russian army's cossacks was fought at this location in 1814. In 1867 under Napoleon III with Baron Haussmann's design, the 60 acres opened as a public park, with a temple to the Roman goddess Sybil crowning the cliff, and caves, waterfalls, lake and rocks hiding old quarry scars. Further adding to its lore, the sound of the French name might suggest an elegance lacking in the English translation of »bald hill«.

Parc Montsouris, 14th arrondissement

The site of Montsouris was chosen to serve the southern area of the city. To the east and west lie the two forests – Vincennes and Boulogne – and to the north Buttes-Chaumont. The park reflects the skill of the Haussmann team in integrating the crossing of two train lines into the design, a practice that continues to be well-employed by contemporary park designers to cover freeways as well as railroad tracks.

The serene green waters here hide deep historical secrets. Use as a stone quarry paved the way for later utilization in the 18th century as catacombs. Reputedly the ossuary received five or six million contributions from ancient cemeteries, deliveries of which were transported by carriage at night through the streets of Paris.

Of particular note among the 1400 trees in the park are the following centenarians: a poplar from Virginia, a cedar of Lebanon, a sequoia from the U.S., two Siberian elms, and a ginkgo biloba. Some 40 species of ducks, geese, swans and migratory birds regularly visit the lake.

Parc Monceau, 8th arrondissement

Edifices envisioned for the elaborate 18th-century amusement of the Duke of Chartres continue to charm visitors. Originally a menagerie of styles, the park featured a windmill, an Egyptian pyramid, a Chinese bridge, an obelisque, a temple to Mars, a minaret, an enchanted cave, an Italian vineyard and castle ruins.

Designed after the English fashion, the park's layout tends to be less formal than the French garden, with curving paths and casual placement of its »follies«. The *pièce de résistance* remains the curved Corinthian colonnaded »La Naumachie« by architect Louis-Marie Colignon.

Once the land became property of the state, Baron Haussmann's architect Gabriel Davidou designed four grand gilded-iron gates and several sculptors fashioned statues to honor such luminaries as Guy de Maupassant, Frédéric Chopin, and Alfred de Musset. Although a shadow of its size while under the duke, the gardens have been embellished by exotic vegetation from England, Austria, Mexico and offer a bonanza of color and variety.

In the late 1800s Claude Monet used the park as the subject matter for five of his Impressionist paintings.

Parc du Ranelagh, an English inspiration, 16th arrondissement

Originally named after an Irish lord, England's famous Ranelagh Gardens opened to the public in 1742. With its open-air rococo rotunda and outdoor hearths, the park quickly became a fashionable music mecca. By 1774 Paris had instituted its own »Petit Ranelagh« devoted to al fresco dance. More than a century later in 1860, the Parc du Ranelagh of Baron Haussmann's design took its place between the palace of La Muette and the village of Passy.

Lined with centuries-old chestnut trees, today's park attracts children both as spectators and active participants with activities ranging from marionettes to donkey rides.

Grand gardens

Although located in three different parts of the city and vastly different in form, size and topography, le Jardin des Champs Elysées, le Jardin du Luxembourg, and les Jardins du Trocadéro share common charms of romantic style, both in building and garden design.

The long, narrow Jardin des Champs Elysées follows the axis from Jardin des Tuileries up to the throng-filled section that is normally associated with the street named after the mythical Greek Elysian Fields. Within steps of the grand boulevard, on both sides, hidden gardens center on fountains, winding bench-lined pathways and floral mosaics.

The Jardin du Luxembourg, the archetypal city park, prizes its sightline that runs from the palace to the Quatre-Parties-du-Monde fountain. Certain aspects of the park evidence its Italian Renaissance past through Marie de Medici.

Les Jardins du Trocadéro, though predating the Tour Eiffel, seem to have been designed specifically for that view. Two wings of the Palais de Chaillot grandly top the hill. Creeks, trees and statues adorn the sides of the hill while the long central, tree-lined fountain gives a sweeping visual introduction to the tower.

Jardin des Champs-Elysées, 8th arrondissement

The Grand Cours, as it was known at first in the 17th century, was created as an extension of the Tuileries by André Le Nôtre. In 1792 ownership was officially transferred from the crown to the public domain. During the Second Empire in the 19th century various theaters, cafés and restaurants were added.

In 1858 the gardens along the Champs-Elysées took on a distinctively more English look under the hand of the engineer Alphand, the director of public works. Giant trees adorned rolling grassways. Rare bushes and baskets of flowers assumed their positions in the foreground.

During the Second Empire under Napoleon III, Baron Haussmann employed foresters, arborists and gardeners to maintain the newly planted landscapes that he had created. In 1868 over 100,000 trees and more than 8000 benches made their appearance along the city's quais and boulevards. The coming of the trees and benches was followed in short order by a fresh discovery – the Parisian love of the promenade.

Strolling the boulevards grew to be *de rigueur*. Suddenly sidewalks offered a new gentility. No matter the weather, there was now a way to walk without the inconvenience of splashing mud and dodging vehicles.

The name Champs-Elysées, or elysian fields, comes from Greek mythology, and means the final resting place for the souls of the heroic and virtuous in Elysium. The 19th-century notion of health spun new meaning into virtue, advocating several hours a day in the parks for the exercise but also to breathe clean, pure air. Paths along planted boulevards, in the gardens, along the lakes led naturally to the advancement of sports.

Jardin du Luxembourg, 6th arrondissement

Home to Romans, monks, Marie de Medici and the Duke of Luxembourg during previous uses, the Luxembourg lands opened to the public in the mid 17th century. Today's gardens bear most the mark of the Medicis, with Marie having chosen and aggrandized the site after tiring of the urban Louvre's location. Particularly the Medici garden reflects the Tuscan flavor she brought to the building and its province. While Luxembourg once represented the Italian Renaissance in France, now it has become central to Parisian life. Its palace still receives dignitaries in impeccably restored senate chambers. Its grounds offer myriad opportunities to learn about horticulture, botany, biohusbandry, and landscape architecture, as well as proffering promenades, cafés, concerts, marionette shows, and other attractions for children's fascination.

Over 600 kinds of apples and pears grow in Luxembourg orchards, as well as Montreuil peaches, prized for centuries. The apiary created in 1856 has been reconstructed in 1991.

A model for New York's Statue of Liberty was presented to Luxembourg gardens by the sculptor Frédéric-Auguste Bartholdi in 1900 and was installed in a corner near Rue Guynemer.

Jardins du Trocadéro, 16th arrondissement, the Roman rocky hill across the Seine

Spilling down the deep slope with sweeping views of the Eiffel Tower the entire way, the gardens at Trocadéro claim a rich past. Chaillot, or »rocky hill« history goes all the way back to the Gallo-Roman era when the ancient village of Nigeon was embraced by the vast Rouvray forest. Later in the Middle Ages the antique manor house in Nigeon belonged to the Dukes of Brittany, and still later to Catherine de Médici who added lavish gardens and terraces. The gardens were designed to be in the English style at the end of the 1800s, with grand trees, rivelets, caves and rustic embellishments.

Napoleon imbued this site with an imperial bearing by honoring the Roman caesars. The name derives from Louis XVIII's 1823 tribute to the conquest of Spain's Trocadero by the Duke of Angoulème.

The palace, which came into being for the 1937 World's Fair, now houses superb museums.

Graceful squares

»Seize every opportunity to place the greatest number of squares possible throughout all the arrondissements of Paris, so that the city can offer graciously as in London, places of relaxation and recreation for all families and all the children, both rich and poor.« Admonition given by Napoléon III, per Baron Haussmann

Square des Batignolles, 17th arrondissement

Complete with cave, cascade, stream, miniature-lake and fragrant trees, this square follows the English, or landscape garden style associated with British landscape architect Capability Brown, with its asymmetric balance, or studied randomness elevating the natural over the artificial. Artifices such as pavilions, domed greenhouses, constructed waterfalls, and rustic concrete bridges showcase the parks' natural aspects. Lawns and pathways are shaded by a variety of trees, including a giant sequoia, purple beech and Japanese persimmon. As in the case of others added to Paris under Emperor Napoléon III, the park was designed by Director of Public Works Jean-Charles Adolphe Alphand, in cooperation with engineer Jean Darcel, architect Gabriel Davidoud and horticulturist Jean-Pierre Barillet-Deschamps.

Until 1860 Batignolles had been an independent village outside Paris when Emperor Napoléon III annexed it to the city. During the 19th century its famous resident painter Edouard Manet (1832 to 1883) led the »groupe des Batignolles« who depicted its vivacious café scene.

Although located a short walk from the new Parc Clichy-Batignolles Martin Luther King, the two are centuries apart in style.

Square du Temple, 3rd arrondissement

Beginning in 1137 the Knights Templar established a Paris presence in a house in the marshland (»marais«) area outside the city walls where the Square du Temple now stands. From then until 1307 they expanded into an area reputedly of about six acres and known as »Villeneuve du Temple«. On Friday the 13th of October of that year the Knights Templar were arrested by then King Philippe le Bel, or Philippe IV, who led an inquisition; the Templars' leader Jacques de Molay was burned at the stake. In the decades that followed, possessions and holdings of the Knights Templar were confiscated or destroyed.

Many of the names in this district bear tribute to the Knights Templar, *Templiers*. The Square du Temple itself was developed in 1857 along with other extensive park development under Napoléon III. Rocks were brought from the Forest of Fontainbleau to construct the waterfall that commands the corner of the park closest to the city hall for the 3rd arrondissement. Gabriel Davidoud designed the iron grillwork that envelops the Square.

Square Louis XVI, 8th arrondissement

Acquired by the city of Paris in 1865, one year after the Boulevard Haussmann sliced through the middle of the original site, this park is situated on a segment of the old cemetery that belonged to the church of the Madeleine. Kitchen gardens for the former bishoperic used to border the property to the north. Louis XVIII arranged for a monument to be constructed here to honor his brother and sister-in-law, Louis XVI and Marie-Antoinette, although their remains were transported to St. Denis for re-burial in 1815.

Square Louvois, 2nd arrondissement

Designated in 1839 as place Richelieu, the Square Louvois was inaugurated in 1859. In 1944 architect Louis Visconti created the centerpiece for the square, an imposing fountain with female figures representing the Seine, the Loire, the Garonne and the Saône rivers. The name derives from the former hotel du marquis de Louvois. In the 17th century the Louvois father and son are credited with having devised measures that increased French military strength but tarnished its humanitarian reputation in Europe.

The square is situated across from the Bibliothèque Nationale, although most of the library's collection was moved to a new complex in the 6th arrondissement in 1996, across the Seine from the Parc de Bercy. The National Library of France was founded originally in 1368 in the Louvre, and expanded and opened to the public in 1692. The reading room at the Richelieu site features a domed ceiling with round windows for natural lighting.

The largest vestige of vast woods

Carpeted with oaks and lilies of the valley, traversed by rivelets and dotted with ponds, the lush green woods of Compiègne have drawn habitants since prehistoric times. The forests saw Julius Caesar's conquests and early Frankish rulers' domains, beginning with Clothaire in the 7th century. Though considerably less than its former magnitude, the extensive woods here still shelter a bounty of animals.

Château de Compiègne, Picardie

Perhaps the most significant portion of the original Rouvray forest that covered the entire area from Compiègne to Roman Lutèce still grows near Compiègne. What may be France's most beautiful woodland still is laced with scenic paths and byways. The forêt de Compiègne contains small villages, Saint-Jean-aux-Bois, Vieux Moulins, and Pierrefonds, that are ideal as rest stops for travelers on bike or foot as well as for evening dining.

Compiègne has been a favored site for regal residences and supreme hunting grounds at least since the 9th century when Charles the Bald built a palace here to resemble Charlemagne's at Aix-la-Chapelle. From that time on a constant stream of royalty found their way to Compiègne, Louis XIV reputedly making 75 visits, and Napoléon III spending four to six weeks here each fall. An 1820s conservatory, built under the water reservoir to supply flowers and plants to the Petit and Grand Parcs, now serves as a museum of Gallic artifacts.

Impressionist artist Maurice Utrillo (1883–1951) often stayed in Saint-Jean-aux-Bois and painted scenes from the picturesque town. Alexandre Dumas (1802–1870) of Picardy used Compiègne as the setting for part of his book *The Count of Monte Cristo*.

A world's fair souvenir

As viewed from above, the field of the Roman god Mars forms a long wide expanse of lawns, with roads striping lengthwise and crosswise and giving grand circular accents. »La Dame de Fer«, as the lattice iron Eiffel Tower is known, reigns over the city as its highest structure, visible from virtually anywhere. The iconic tower and its green stage came into being as part of the 1889 Exposition Universelle, or World's Fair, replacing former military installations.

Parc du Champ-de-Mars, 7th arrondissement

If one image remains synonymous with Paris, it must be the Tour Eiffel. Rising on a bank of the Seine, visible across long swaths of great green lawns and down steep staircases, glimpsed from almost anywhere, it seems, and able to be reached en masse on foot from essentially all directions, the tower stands as a world symbol of the grace and elegance comfortably at home in Paris. Like a gem, its setting adds to its value. From its base, grand parks extend their green arms toward the horizons: up to Trocadéro, ancient hillside across the Seine; along Champs-de-Mars, flat with its lawns and fields. Shaded walkways along the Seine offer miles of clear views. Motionless bridges span quick-paced currents offering vistas in mobile contexts.

Named after its designer Gustave Eiffel, the tallest building in Paris stands not only as the most recognized monument in the world. At its feet stretch the most visited fields of the Roman god of war, the Champs-de-Mars, unfurling southeastward from the river to the Ecole Militaire.

The site was chosen and prepared to host the World's Fairs of 1867. The tower was built as the gateway to the 1889 World's Fair and to celebrate the centennial of the French Revolution.

The grounds opened to the public in 1780; the army fully ceded the property to the city of Paris in 1889 in exchange for land in Issy-les-Moulineaux, a southwestern suburb.

The wide fields attract soccer games and other sports. A bandstand draws constant crowds in warm weather, and the marionette theatre remains a favorite activity for all ages. Pines, gingkos and tulip trees, as well as cedars from Lebanon and China proffer stately shade.

Island promenades

Slipping out of the city scene into a green refuge may be superb in itself, but adding the buffeting effect of water has to be sublime. Much like moats around a castle, the river shields these parks from casual intrusions. The water acts as a barrier without being visually obstructive; bridges allow access.

The islands in the Seine mentioned here give a small glimpse into the distinctive character of their promenades. One long-standing and artificially formed and one newly transformed from military to public use, each affords lovely strolls.

Allée des Cygnes, 15th/16th arrondissement

The Allée des Cygnes refers to the pathway down the middle of the island park known as the Ile des Cygnes. Created in 1827 the long thin slice of land serves as a breakwater to shield the port of Grenelle. Another island by the same

name further to the north in the Seine no longer exists.

Whether stepping down in the middle of the Seine from the elegant, chandelier-bedecked bridge of Bir-Hakeim at the north end, or climbing up to the Grenelle bridge at the south end near the Radio France complex, a stroll in the middle of the slim island seems miles removed from the urban rush. Although the Eiffel Tower rises majestically just across the Seine, the multitudes that collect at its base rarely reach this locally-favored retreat.

Ile de St. Germain, Issy les Moulineaux, Hauts-de-Seine

To the southwest of Paris, just outside the Périphérique and before the river loops back to the north, l'Ile de St. Germain occupies its thin sliver of the Seine. At the beginning of the 1980s, pastoral public lands with an array of walking paths started to take the place of former military grounds here. The main part is comprised of a natural garden intended for biodiversity studies, with one area devoted to a three-story A-frame pony stable building. Part of the island of St. Germain contains offices and housing, with spaces dedicated to art and architecture studios.

In the spring pink roses bedeck wooden fences that bound a picturesque country lane. Several artistic artifices – some pillared – showcase grapevines and enclosed gardens. The colorfully painted sculpture *La Tour aux Figures* by Jean Dubuffet (1901–1985) was inaugurated in the park as a historical monument in 1988.

Artists' gifts to the ages

Art needs beauty to breathe. It falls on the sensitive few to guard the phenomenal, to keep the flame, to protect the treasures. Artists have saved Fontainebleau, created gallery gardens and rescued abbeys. Artists show the inner eye why to preserve.

This section pays homage to a representative few of those who have followed the green muse.

Fôret de Fontainebleau, Seine-et-Marne

In the mid-19th-century artists painting en plein-air in Barbizon banded together to save a favorite subject from being loved to death. Their efforts preserved Fontainebleau.

The weapons were paintbrushes, conservation the campaign. Théodore Rousseau led the charge. It didn't start as a struggle.

As many other artists of the day, Camille Corot began by studying Renaissance masters in Italy. There he learned how to portray light, sky and rock. Memories of Fontainebleau beckoned him back to paint en plein-air.

Within a short time an artist colony collected in neighboring Barbizon. In a break from tradition, the artists moved the background to the fore in their work; landscape became recognized as a subject for its own sake.

In 1852 Théodore Rousseau petitioned Emperor Napoleon III to protect the forest as a nature

8. Édouard André, *Le jardin de roses*, L'Haÿ, Val-de-Marne, 1902.
9. Claude Monet, *Le Déjeuner sur l'herbe*, 1865/1866. From: Chantal Georgel, *La forêt de Fontainebleau. Un atelier grandeur nature*, Editions de la Réunion des musées nationaux, Paris, 2007, p. 98.
10. Paul Cézanne, *Rochers dans le bois*. 1893. From: Chantal Georgel, op. cit., p. 61.
11. Camille Corot, *Détails de troncs d'arbres en forêt*, 1822. From: Chantal Georgel, op. cit., p. 33.

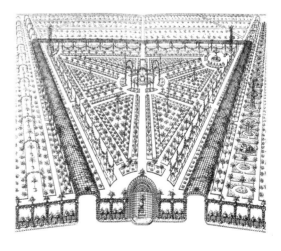

preserve. By 1861 the petition was granted in large part, making Fontainebleau the world's first national forest.

The arts forged a powerful alliance with parklands in Fontainebleau. France sets the gold standard in the world of natural art.

The artist colony at Barbizon, Seine-et-Marne

The allure of plein-air painting in Fontainebleau drew Gustave Courbet, Jean-François Millet, Frederic Bazille, Narcisse Diaz de la Peña, Auguste Renoir, Alfred Sisley and Théodore Rousseau to Barbizon. A natural gathering place for painters, the quaint stone cottages that clustered together in the small village saw most of France's finest talent pass through. For half a century or so the colony enjoyed its full bloom, and even today some of the local businesses still display artists' work accepted in trade for food or lodging.

Monet's art gardens

Nowhere does the line between art and nature become less distinguishable than in Monet's gardens in Giverny. Bare land became Claude Monet's blank canvas. The play of color from flowers to pond, the effects of light and shadow, and the intensity of hues all combine to transport Giverny beyond the imperfections of reality and into a fantasy realm. Ramblers through the gardens become part of a grand Impressionistic painting.

Monet's inspirations and actions, from Fontainebleau to Giverny, Eure

Fellow artists' activism at Fontainebleau and Barbizon profoundly affected Oscar Claude Monet. In Paris he had established professional friendships with Alfred Sisley, Auguste Renoir and Frédéric Bazille. In 1863 Monet led them to Fontainebleau to further their painting techniques, which had been influenced considerably by English landscape artist and master of light and water portrayals, Joseph Mallord William Turner.

Just north of Barbizon, Chailly-en-Bière drew Monet repeatedly to paint en plein-air and to infuse more openness and light into his painting. Striving to show reality in nature rather than classical perfection, he set up his huge 15 by 20 foot canvas in the woods and began registering nature's wonders in a whole new way. A picnic attended by an elegantly-dressed group of diners entitled *Dejéuner sur l'herbe*, was painted outdoors in the forest of Fontainebleau in 1855 or 1856; about a dozen other of his pieces were also painted in the vicinity.

In 1883 Monet looked out the window of a train and fell in love with Giverny. Driven to grow and create his own subject matter for his painting, he acquired a piece of property there and diverted a stream to nourish his project. Some of his most famous paintings derive from Giverny, especially involving the lily ponds, bridges and trellises.

Claude Monet had settled in Giverny after spending time in Fontainebleau. Almost immediately artists began congregating there, much as

artists before them had been drawn to Fontainebleau. For about 30 years from 1885 until World War I a group of American artists including Willard Metcalf, Louis Ritter, Theodore Wendel, and John Leslie Breck, Theodore Robinson, Frederick Mac-Monnies, Theodore Butler, Louis Paul Dessar, Richard Emil Miller Frederick, Carl Frieseke, William Blair Bruce and Alson Clark gathered in Giverny. From 1860 to 1930 spending time in France was considered *de rigueur* for any aspiring American artist.

A major champion of Impressionism, art dealer Durand-Ruel, arranged exhibits of Monet's work in New York. As Impressionistic works became known, a strong network of support developed on the East Coast. Both artists and patrons regularly visited Giverny.

In 1926 Monet died, but his work still resides in the enchanted setting that he crafted in Giverny. In 1966 his only heir Michel bequeathed his father's art and property to the French academy of fine arts, part of the Institut de France. Monet's contribution to the art world and to France remains immeasurable; his work ushered in the new era of Impressionism and his family made it possible for the gardens to continue to be public.

Musée des Impressionnismes and its gardens in Giverny, Eure

In a story that links Chicago with Giverny and America with Impressionism, chemistry student Daniel Terra discovered an ink to speed the operation of printing presses, which in turn led to the production of the first photo-illustrated *Life* magazine. With funds borrowed from his friend John Lawson he formed Lawter Chemical, a leading producer of printing inks and chemicals. His marriage to painter Adeline Richards, their subsequent art collecting in Chicago and their joint commitment to American art inspired the formation of both the Terra Museum of American Art in Chicago in 1987 and the Musée d'Art Américain in Giverny in 1992.

The portraitist's abbey of Chaalis, Oise

The romance of Nélie Jacquemart provides the perfect segue between art and abbey, Paris and its spheres. An accomplished portrait painter with canny and wherewithal, she acquired and preserved Chaalis abbey. At that time her Paris home already had been consecrated for use as a museum.

Fate smiled on France the day Ms. Jacquemart arrived at Edouard André's mansion on Boulevard Haussmann in the 8th arrondissement and the world at large continues to reap the benefits. Ms. Jacquemart married Mr. André and counseled him on the acquisition of their splendid art collection from all over the world. Much of the collection continues on public display in what had been their finely appointed private home.

After her husband died, Ms. Jacquemart expanded her sights beyond Paris and purchased an abbey originally dating back to the 12th century. Although the cathedral remains in ruins, many of the other buildings have been restored and a charming walled roseraie reestablished. Situated to the northeast of Paris near Ermenonville, Chaalis held special significance for Ms. Jacquemart because she had grown up in the surrounding area.

As agreed with her husband, she gave their city home to the Institut de France for use as a museum and it opened in 1913. Nélie Jacquemart also gave the abbey to the Institut de France for use as a museum to house part of the couple's art collection.

Rodin's bequests of his work and two museums

Musée Rodin in Paris, 7th arrondissement

Sculptor of international renown Auguste Rodin conferred upon the French government the gift of all his masterpieces. The sculptures comprise an invaluable acquisition for France; his gift of the museums to display them has enabled his work to survive him in a remarkable way. In Paris and Meudon his art lives on in garden settings he chose and preserved.

Rodin (1840–1917) had lived in the little town of Meudon, to the southwest of Paris. In 1908 he rented a Parisian manor house recently acquired by the French government called Hôtel Biron. Immediately he set about turning Biron into a museum to house his imposing marble statues.

Since 1919 le Jardin du Musée Rodin with its extensive grounds in the 7th arrondissement has served as museum and park. A short distance from the Champs-de-Mars and Esplanade des Invalides, as well as the market street of Rue Cler, it sits quietly several blocks behind the Musée d'Orsay. Inside the gate, however, the visitor feels transported to another dimension both because of the Rodin figures but also because of the intricacy of the setting.

Al-fresco galleries enclosed in hedges allow separate viewings for individual masterpieces. Bronze figures assume greater-than-human attributes in their portrayal of unfiltered emotion. The classical green setting is superbly tailored to its supporting role; allées of linden and maple add statuesque proportion; apple, plum and cherries bring fullness and life.

Not only did Rodin succeed in bringing realism to the art of sculpture, a world that before then had been tied to allegorical and mythological subjects. He also insured that his work be shown in two museums for succeeding generations. Together the Jardin du Musée Rodin and the Musée Rodin in Meudon display the majority of his work.

Musée Rodin in Meudon, Hauts-de-Seine

It seems only fitting that the northwest part of August Rodin's hometown that looks down at the Seine would be named »Bellevue«, or beautiful view. The façade of his villa, Les Brillants, was taken from the old palace of neighboring Issy-les-Moulineaux; a public exhibition of his sculpture is housed in the villa. Since the time Rodin sculpted here in the early 20th century, the area has held an allure for artists and composers, including Alsatian

sculptor Jean Arp whose former home studio displays his work.

Sandwiched between a south loop of the Seine and the Forêt de Meudon, the town linked to Versailles by a forest road that used to be an ancient royal route, or Pavé des Gardes. In its 17th-century heyday under Louis XIV, Meudon drew considerable attention as the residence of the dauphin. André Le Nôtre's original landscape design can be detected from the terrace that remains of the Bellevue palace overlooking the Seine valley.

The name Meudon itself derives from the Gallic word for sand dune, but signs of habitation reach back to the Neolithic era.

Private benefactors' gardens. Reaping the rich dividends of financial success and passion

Today's visitors may enjoy enhanced and singular experiences thanks to two wealthy 20th-century purveyors. Each cherished roses, gardens and carefully crafted floral havens. Each chose a site just outside Paris and created nirvanas on lands that are now open to the public.

Gravereaux' roseraies

After retiring from his position as head of Bon Marché, Jules Gravereaux began expanding his rose collection at his home in L'Haÿ just south of Paris. He had acquired the remainder of Josephine Bonaparte's garden, probably fewer than 50 plants. Soon the number swelled to the thousands.

In 1900 the commissioner of gardens for the city of Paris engaged Mr. Gravereaux to create a rose garden for Bagatelle in the Bois de Boulogne. By 1909 he undertook one at Malmaison, home of Josephine's original roses. L'Haÿ, known as Laiacum in Charlemagne's era, previously the estate of Gallo-Roman Lagius, officially became »L'Haÿ-les-Roses« in 1914 in honor of the splendors wrought there.

All three gardens – Roseraie du Val-de-Marne, as L'Haÿ is known, Rueil-Malmaison to the west of Paris, and Bagatelle in the heart of the Bois de Boulogne – trace their existence to the early 20th-century efforts of Mr. Gravereaux. In May probably the first and most spectacular shows can be seen, although throughout the spring, summer and fall certain varieties may be in bloom. All three rose gardens adjoin parks of varying size.

Albert Kahn, musée et jardins, Boulogne-Billancourt, Hauts-de-Seine

Until Wall Street crashed in 1929, the national Albert Kahn museum and gardens belonged to a renowned financier and proponent of peace. Now located in the town renamed Boulogne-Billancourt along the Seine and just west and slightly south of Paris, Kahn's home had served as a frequent gathering place for European interlligensia; at the time Boulogne beckoned Parisians to retreat the short distance down the Seine from Paris.

12. Claude Monet, *Nymphéas*, 1908. From: Marina Ferretti Bocquillon (ed.), *Le jardin de Monet à Giverny: l'invention d'un paysage*, Musée des Impressionnismes, Giverny, 2009, p. 77.
13. Claude Monet, *Iris jaunes*, 1924/25. From: Marina Ferretti Bocquillon, op. cit., p. 24.

Until 1924 the French commune had been named Boulogne-sur-Seine and held about half of the Bois de Boulogne within its boundaries; in 1929 the city of Paris annexed all of the Bois de Boulogne. At the time the area drew artists and writers; it also served as the birthplace of the cinema, automobile and aircraft industries. The proximity to Auguste Rodin's home in Meudon facilitated the fast friendship between the artist and Kahn.

On his lands, Kahn created a harmonious blend of diverse landscapes: a roseraie, a Japanese tearoom and its gardens, a conifer wood and an English garden. He promoted scholarship, especially in his project that sent photographers into all parts of the world in an innovative early use of color photography, autochrome plates, and cinematography.

His pictorial record from 50 countries constitutes »The Archives of the Planet« and can be viewed at the Kahn museum; his photographic collection from 1914 was compiled in conjunction with the French military and documents the disasters of war and the ensuing human tragedies. Kahn died as a victim of World War II.

20th- and 21st-century Parisian make-overs. From Eyesore to Eden

As an integral part of urban design, park planning keeps Paris green. Function, scale, proportion, circulation and orientation all go into the formation and preservation of open spaces. The process involves excavation, engineering, electricity, plumbing, horticulture and agriculture.

In addition to including park planning in its curriculum for higher education in France, programs are staged in the parks to instruct the public about park design, construction and management. Science continues to be emphasized, both within the parks once completed as in the initial creation. Concepts of outdoor rooms and halls relate to uses envisioned for the spaces.

Park design anticipates myriad activities and recreational possibilities. Strolling, boating, biking, skating, riding, ball playing, birding, swimming, dining, reading, sketching and viewing all fit into the scheme of contemplated uses. Down to the benches and fencing materials, design is individualized to the specific place. Maintenance and adjusting to seasonal changes and demands must be built into the park's concepts as well, and funds allotted regularly for those purposes. The greening of Paris includes the planting of trees along even the narrowest of streets. Whatever the size – bois, parc, jardin or square – the parks are Parisian treasures that the rest of the world is privileged to share.

Parc de la Villette, 19th arrondissement

An example of a modern make-over from a former abbatoir, this urban park designed by architect Bernard Tschumi inaugurated in the 1970s offers a panoply of activities and fascination. Bright red follies pepper the park with interest. Big box-shaped contrivances feature architectural curiosities like water wheels, step-down cascades and corkscrew staircases. The park bridges the Canal de l'Ourco with large lawns on both sides; ferries shuttle in and out. The vast entry square centers on a fountain and a long pavilion, with a hall of science and industry, performance hall and café nearby.

Parc de Belleville, 20th arrondissement

On one of the highest hills in Paris, exceeding even Montmartre, a surprisingly new park offers inside views that are as charming as its more distant vistas. Gently curving pathways wind through enchantingly landscaped bowers. Planted staircases, key features on this steep slope, pose as careful compositions.

Many natural springs originate in Belleville and typically have fed other parts of Paris.

In the Roman era water was channelled to other locations from this source. Even now Belleville claims the grandest cascading fountain in Paris.

Although opened to the public in 1988, the location of Belleville has played an important, if not uninterrupted, part in French history since the Romans. The hill was considered to be so highly desirable that both the Mérovingians (5th- to 8th-century rulers) and Carolingians (8th- and 9th-century rulers) chose the site as a royal residence. Before the 13th century the hill was known as Savies, and until the 16th century as Pointronville. This vantage point has given strategic advantage throughout history to those who held it.

Promenade plantée and Reuilly, 12th arrondissement

Since the early 1990s Parisians have been able to take a three-mile walk through a narrow garden in one of the busiest parts of the city without stopping for a single traffic light. Towers of roses, bright-faced flowerbeds and garden arcades accompany travelers along the path. Designed on a former elevated railway track, the high walkway runs from the Bastille to the Périphérique.

The vantage point above street level offers a different perspective of stately residences, shops, markets and inner courtyards along the way. Here and there benches set the scene for a pause or refreshment. A dedicated bicycle trail begins from the vintage rail station of Reuilly.

Seven geographic sequences grace the trail, with both evergreen and perennial vegetation. Two newer parks link directly with the Promenade: the Jardin de Reuilly and the Square Charles-Péguy. A few steps from the Bastille-end of the park lies the Jardin de l'Arsenal, affording a pleasant walk along the boat harbor; a few steps south from the eastern end leads to the Bois de Vincennes.

Jardin de Reuilly, 12th arrondissement

Fanning out midway along the Promenade plantée, Reuilly's green space adds breathing room for hikers. Sitting high over the busy streets below, it feels like a hilltop retreat. Especially the expansive circular lawn radiates an air of neighborhood meeting place.

From a historical perspective this site holds some significance, despite the recent 1992 vintage of the park itself. Reuilly, a Mérovingian ruler's Paris residence, was located here.

Parc de Bercy, 12th arrondissement

If Bercy brings to mind the Tuileries it is by no accident. The location of this new 1990s park was chosen to balance the city's distribution of parklands. Accordingly the Bercy area south on the Seine possesses its own Tuileries, somewhat similar to the one further north.

The long linear look of Bercy may also suggest an earlier reliance on access to the Seine, at least with regards to the industrial part of its past. Old rail lines imbedded in cobblestone walkways used to haul railcars filled with wine barrels back and forth from river barges in the 19th-century days as a warehouse depot. Vineyards in today's park pay tribute to past usage, and even yield enough grapes for bottling.

Evidencing an even more distant time, the centenarian trees once graced a palace here, with gardens designed by André Le Nôtre. A 17th-century vine-covered building dates from the time that a château sat amidst extensive gardens. Courtyards now host avid gardeners at city-sponsored open houses.

In vegetable gardens small signs identify plants throughout various stages of development. A fragrance garden includes white wisteria covered-trellises; a labyrinth and roseraie add an air of antiquity. The high promenade overlooking the river features sculptures of children from around the world. The green roofed stadium melds into the park landscape.

Parc André-Citroën, 15th arrondissement

Reflecting its former industrial use as car manufacturing plant, Citroën sits along a working quai of the Seine with trains running by every few minutes. Inaugurated only in 1992, the park's youth corresponds to the newness of the surrounding area of hospital, office and apartment buildings. A long central plaza perpendicular to the river contains a fountain; two graceful glass conservatories rise at the opposite end. Walkways and flowerbeds flank the plaza on either side. A wilderness garden enables studies of natural progressions.

Jardin Atlantique, 15th arrondissement

Held by twelve colossal concrete arches, a vast suspended platform floats over the rails leading to Montparnasse station. On its surface, tennis courts and ping-pong tables are placed in areas too shallow for tree roots due to the ventilation systems just below; in between, hundreds of parking places have been layered. Engineering feats aside, Atlantique looks like a typically beautiful Paris park.

The Atlantique carries out an ocean theme in design and vegetation. The long central Alleé des Métamorphoses attracts not only young skaters but also the travelers who ride up the escalator from Montparnasse station. The surrounding high-

rise development underwrote some park costs in obtaining its building permit; its employees have been reaping the benefits of extra breathing and recreation space since 1994.

Musée du quai Branly, wetlands and Promenade du quai Branly, 7th arrondissement

Between the Pont de l'Alma and the Pont de Bir-Hakeim in the 15th arrondissement the Branly promenade runs along the banks of the Seine River and across the street from the Branly museum and café, which opened in 2006. Known for its living wall façade that resembles a tapestry of plant material, the Branly gardens also feature wetlands. Functioning as a modern moat, the expanse of water between the street and museum impedes unwelcome visits while providing ecological benefits and visual interest.

A nascent park: Parc Clichy-Batignolles Martin Luther King, 17th arrondissement

Like most construction projects, park creation begins with plans – for excavating, pipe-laying, reservoir building, then planting, watering, fountains, walkways and benches.

Plants and trees are chosen and placed with an eye toward their appearance five years later; that is, five years after the planting has been done, a park will reach its optimal stage of development. Water features play an important role and, especially in newer parks, rainwater is collected and recycled.

The public works department of the mayor's office sets up project headquarters on site and selects materials. Colors, railing decor and themes relate to the specific place. For Clichy-Batignolles, each of the park's quadrants represents a different season of the year, and there are also visual references to past use as rail yards.

The area had been set aside as housing for Olympic athletes, but was allocated for parkland after France lost its bid to host the 2012 Olympics.

Parc Georges-Brassens, 15th arrondissement

The air cleared and a fresh new day dawned when the last remnants of the stockyards disappeared from the village of Vaugirard in the mid-1970s. In their place vineyards and beehives reclaimed spaces occupied in prior eras, and blocks from demolished buildings took on the new form of community playground.

Named after its famous resident bard Georges Brassens (1921–1981), the park's spaces seem to have taken on a lyrical quality, from the old belfry tower to the traditional Saturday Guignol puppet shows under the shelter of a modern pavilion. Renown all over France for his chansons, Brassens revived the words penned by medieval poet François Villon, 19th-century author Victor Hugo, and 20th-century poet Paul Verlaine, setting to music their themes of love, death and individualism.

References

General

Bührer-Thierry, Geneviève, *L'Europe carolingienne (714–888)*, Armand Colin, Paris, 2004.

Ferretti Bocquillon, Marina (ed.), *Le jardin de Monet à Giverny: l'invention d'un paysage*, Musée des Impressionnismes, Giverny, 2009.

Gouguenheim, Sylvain, *Regards sur le Moyen Âge*, Tallandier, Paris, 2009.

Landsberg, Sylvia, *The Medieval Garden*, University of Toronto Press, Toronto, 2003.

Liddiard, Robert, *The Medieval Park: New Perspectives*, Windgather Press Ltd., Cheshire, 2007.

Lorentz, Philippe, and Dany Sandron, *Atlas de Paris au Moyen Âge: espace urbain, habitat, société, religion, lieux de pouvoir*, Parigramme, Paris, 2006.

Mariage, Thierry, *The World of André le Nôtre*, translated by Graham Larkin, University of Pennsylvania Press, 1999. Originally published as *L'univers de la Nostre*, Éditions Mardaga, Wavre, Belgium, 1990.

Pinon, Pierre, *Atlas du Paris haussmannien: La ville en heritage du Second Empire à nos jours*, Parigramme, Paris, 2002.

Pitt, Leonard, *Paris. A journey through time*, Counterpoint, Berkeley, 2010.

Poisson, Georges, *Histoire et histoires de Sceaux. Les amis du Musée de l'Ile de France*, Château de Sceaux, 1981.

Strabo, *Geographica*, originally an 17-volume work by Greek historian, philosopher and geographer from the beginning of the current era; eight volumes available in translation by Horace Leonard Jones from the 1930s and the 1950s.

The Song of Roland, translated by Dorothy Sayers, Penguin Books, Middlesex, 1957; *La chanson de Roland. Lettres gothiques*, edition critique et traduction de Ian Short, Le Livre de Poche, Paris, 1990.

Williamson, John, *The Oak King, the Holly King, and the Unicorn: The Myths and Sybolism of the Unicorn Tapestries*, Harper & Row, New York, 1986.

Parks and gardens

Alphand, Jean-Charles-Adolphe, *Les promenades de Paris*, J. Rothschild, Paris, 1867–1873.

Babelon, Jean-Pierre, and Jean-Marc Vasseur, *L'abbaye royale de Chaalis et les collections Jacquemart-André*, Editions du Patrimoine, Paris, 2007.

Barozzi, Jacques, *Guide des 400 jardins publics de Paris*, Editions Hervas, Paris, 1992.

Chantal Georgel, *La Forêt de Fontainebleau. Un atelier grandeur nature,* Editions de la Réunion des musées nationaux, Paris, 2007.

Gousset, Marie-Thérèse, *Jardins médiévaux en France, itinéraires de découvertes*, Editions Ouest-France, Rennes, 2003.

Hervet, Jean-Pierre, and Patrick Mérienne, *La Forêt de Fontainebleau. Et les forêts des Trois-Pignons, de Barbeau et de Larchant-La Commanderie*, Office National des Forêts, Editions Ouest-France, Rennes, 2009.

Jarrassé, Dominique, *Grammaire des jardins parisiens*, Parigramme, Paris, 2007.

MacDougall, Elisabeth Blair (ed.), *Medieval Gardens*, Dumbarton Oaks Research Library and Collection, Washington, D.C., 1986.

Moncan, Patrice de, *Paris, les jardins d'Haussmann*, Les Editions du Mécène, Paris, 2009.

1. Square du Vert-Galant, 1st arrondissement
(p. 11).
2. Les Arènes de Lutèce, 5th arrondissement
(p. 11).

3. Cluny gardens, 5th arrondissement (p. 11).
Medieval-style section.
4. Square René Le Gall, 13th arrondissement
(p. 12).

5. Jardin des Plantes, 5th arrondissement (p. 12). Allée.
6. Jardin des Plantes, 5th arrondissement. Canopy detail.
7. Jardin des Plantes, 5th arrondissement. Grand Galerie.

8. Jardin des Tuileries, 1st arrondissement (p. 13). Allée with café.
9. Jardin des Tuileries, 1st arrondissement. Promenade along the Seine.
10. Jardin des Tuileries, 1st arrondissement. Elevated-walkway with the Louvre in the background.

15. Château de Fontainebleau, Seine-et-Marne.
(p. 13). Entry gate.
16. Château de Fontainebleau, Seine-et-Marne.
Axis.

17. Château de Fontainebleau, Seine-et-Marne.
View across the lake.

18. Château de Fontainebleau, Seine-et-Marne.
Fountains and cone trees.
19. Château de Fontainebleau, Seine-et-Marne.
Statue of Diana from 1603.

20. Château de St. Germain-en-Laye, Yvelines (p. 14). The castle.
21. Château de St. Germain-en-Laye, Yvelines. Le Nôtre terrace.
22. Château de St. Germain-en-Laye, Yvelines. Cone tree-lined allée against backdrop of Paris skyline.

23. Château de Vaux le Vicomte, Seine-et-Marne (p. 14). The castle.
24. Château de Vaux le Vicomte, Seine-et-Marne. Sculpted hedges.
25. Château de Vaux le Vicomte. Landscaping against forest backdrop.

26. Château de Vaux le Vicomte, Seine-et-Marne.
Landscape by Le Nôtre.
27. Château de Vaux le Vicomte, Seine-et-Marne.
Landscape with castle.

p. 50/51
28. Château de Versailles, Yvelines (p. 14). Main
axis.

29. Château de Versailles, Yvelines. Round pool.
30. Château de Versailles, Yvelines. Orangerie,
parterre.

31. Château de Versailles, Yvelines. Urns on pedestals.

pp. 56/57
32. Château de Sceaux, Hauts-de-Seine (p. 14).
Axis.

33. Château de Sceaux, Hauts-de-Seine. Castle
through the conifers, hedging.
34. Château de Sceaux, Hauts-de-Seine. Castle
with cone trees.
35. Château de Sceaux, Hauts-de-Seine. Canal,
forests and balustrade.

36. Château de Saint-Cloud, Hauts-de-Seine
(p. 15).
37. Château de Saint-Cloud, Hauts-de-Seine.
Balustraded pond and lawns.

38. Château de Saint-Cloud, Hauts-de-Seine.
Grande Cascade.
39. Château de Saint-Cloud Hauts-de-Seine.
Frog sculptures.
40. Château de Saint-Cloud, Hauts-de-Seine.
Grande Cascade, upper level.

41. Château de Meudon, Hauts-de-Seine (p. 15).
42. Château de Chantilly, Oise (p. 15).

43. Château de Chantilly, Oise. Castle and grounds.
44. Château de Chantilly, Oise. Grand canal.
45. Château de Chantilly, Oise. Castle, moat and forest.

46. Palais Royal, 1st arrondissement (p. 15).
47. Palais Royal, 1st arrondissement. Tree hedging.
48. Palais Royal, 1st arrondissement. Lawns and flower-bed bouquets.

49. Square Louis XIII, Place des Vosges, 3rd arrondissement (p. 16).
50. Square Louis XIII, Place des Vosges, 3rd arrondissement. Fountain, sand playground.

pp. 72/73
51. Square Louis XIII, Place des Vosges, 3rd arrondissement. Benches in linden bosquet.

pp. 74/75
52. Bois de Boulogne, 16th arrondissement
(p. 16). Oak archway.

53. Bois de Boulogne, 16th arrondissement.
Chalet des Iles.
54. Bois de Boulogne, 16th arrondissement.
Orangerie in the Parc de Bagatelle.
55. Bois de Boulogne, 16th arrondissement.
Jardin Shakespeare.

56. Bois de Boulogne, 16th arrondissement.
Grande Cascade.
57. Bois de Boulogne, 16th arrondissement.
Concrete-sculpted bridge railing in rustic
horned style.

58. Bois de Boulogne, 16th arrondissement.
Gilded entry gate.
59. Bois de Boulogne, 16th arrondissement.
Bagatelle garden-house pathway.
60. Bois de Boulogne, 16th arrondissement.
Bench in hedgeway niche.

61. Bois de Vincennes, 12th arrondissement
(p. 17). Lac Daumesnil.
62. Bois de Vincennes, 12th arrondissement.
Lac Daumesnil, Ile de Reuilly.

63. Bois de Vincennes, 12th arrondissement.
Lac Daumesnil, Ile de Bercy.
64. Bois de Vincennes, 12th arrondissement.
Parc Floral water lilly ponds.

65. Bois de Vincennes, 12th arrondissement.
Parc Floral performance pavilion.
66. Bois de Vincennes, 12th arrondissement.
The park's signature sign posts.

67. Parc des Buttes-Chaumont, 10th arrondissement (p. 17). Belvedere of Sybil.
68. Parc des Buttes-Chaumont, 10th arrondissement. Grotto with waterfall.

69. Parc des Buttes-Chaumont, 10th arrondissement. Limestone cliff with Belvedere.
70, 71. Parc des Buttes-Chaumont, 10th arrondissement. Napoléon III-Haussmann restaurants.

72. Parc Montsouris, 14th arrondissement (p. 17).
Reservoir covering past entrance to catacombs.
73. Parc Montsouris, 14th arrondissement. Weather
station.

74. Parc Monceau, 8th arrondissement (p. 17). Colonnaded naumachie.
75. Parc Monceau, 8th arrondissement. Approximate location of one of Claude Monet's Parc Monceau paintings.

76. Parc du Ranelagh, 16th arrondissement, (p. 17). Statue portraying La Fontaine and a fox and raven, characters from one of his fables.
77. Parc du Ranelagh, 16th arrondissement. Fall-bronzed chestnut trees and blue pavilion.

pp. 98/99
78. Jardin des Champs-Elysées, 8th arrondissement, (p. 18). Promenade toward Théâtre Marigny.

79. Jardin des Champs-Elysées, 8th arrondissement. California sequoia given by America to France
in 1989, commemorating 200 years of human rights
and friendship (to the right of the pathway).
80. Jardin des Champs-Elysées, 8th arrondissement. Rond-point.
81. Jardin des Champs-Elysées, 8th arrondissement. 19th-century pavilion behind rond-point.

82. Jardin des Champs-Elysées, 8th arrondissement. Near Cours la Reine, bronze beech tree and
fountain after Roman goddess Diana.
83. Jardin des Champs-Elysées, 8th arrondissement. 19th-century bandstand.

84. Jardin du Luxembourg, 6th arrondissement (p. 18). Italianate palace commissioned by Marie de Medici.
85. Jardin du Luxembourg, 6th arrondissement. Ballustraded terrace.
86. Jardin du Luxembourg, 6th arrondissement. Fontaine des Quatre-Parties-du-Monde, also known as the Fontaine de l'Observatoire, or Fontaine Carpeaux.

87. Jardin du Luxembourg, 6th arrondissement.
Lawn ringed by rounded topiaries.
88. Jardin du Luxembourg, 6th arrondissement.
Cupids holding bouquet-like pot of flowers.

89. Jardin du Luxembourg, 6th arrondissement.
Statute giving hommage to a poet.
90. Jardin du Luxembourg, 6th arrondissement.
Fontaine Medici.

91. Jardin du Luxembourg, 6th arrondissement.
Le pavilion de la fontaine.
92. Jardins du Trocadéro, 16th arrondissement
(p. 18).

93. Jardins du Trocadéro, 16th arrondissement.
View of 25 rue Benjamin Franklin by Auguste
Perret.
94. Square des Batignolles, 17th arrondissement
(p. 18). In the English romantic style.

95. Square du Temple, 3rd arrondissement (p. 19).
From the 19th-century Napoléon III-Haussman era.
96. Square Louis XVI, 8th arrondissement (p. 19).

97. Square Louvois, 2nd arrondissement, (p. 19).
19th-century Napoléon III-Haussman grillwork.
98. Square Louvois, 2nd arrondissement. Fontaine
Louvois representing the four rivers Seine, Loire,
Saône and Garonne.

99, 100. Château de Compiègne, Picardie (p. 19).
L'allée des Beaux Monts with Compiègne-style
sign posts.

101. Château de Compiègne, Picardie. Saint-Jean-aux-Bois.
102. Château de Compiègne, Picardie. Pierrefonds.
103. Château de Compiègne, Picardie. Maison forestière.

106. Parc Ile de St. Germain, Issy les Moulineaux,
Hauts-de-Seine, (p. 20).
107. Parc Ile de St. Germain, Issy les Moulineaux,
Hauts-de-Seine. Blue folly.

pp. 126/127
108. Forêt de Fontainebleau, Seine-et-Marne
(p. 20). Ferns and famous rocks.

109, 110. Forêt de Fontainebleau, Seine-et-Marne.
Animal-like rock formations.

108. Forêt de Fontainebleau, Seine-et-Marne
(p. 20). Ferns and famous rocks.

111. Forêt de Fontainebleau, Seine-et-Marne. Rock cave.
112. Forêt de Fontainebleau, Seine-et-Marne. White birch.

113. Forêt de Fontainebleau, Seine-et-Marne.
Luminescent forest floor.
114. Moret-sur-Loing, Seine-et-Marne. Village
near Fontainebleau where Barbizon Alfred Sisley
painted and resided.

115. Monet's garden in Giverny, Eure, Haute-Normandie (p. 21). Green bridge and ponds, subjects of Claude Monet's paintings.
116. Monet's garden in Giverny, Eure, Haute-Normandie. Garden walkways along ponds.

117. Monet's garden in Giverny, Eure, Haute-Normandie. Iris-lined path to Claude Monet's home.
118. Monet's garden in Giverny, Eure, Haute-Normandie. Low-slung rose archways.

119. Monet's garden in Giverny, Eure, Haute-Normandie. View of Monet's home from the street.
120. Musée des Impressionnismes in Giverny,
Eure, Haute-Normandie (p. 21). Sculpted hedge
entry with white wisteria.

121. Abbaye de Chaalis, Fontaine-Chaalis, near Ermenonville, Oise (p. 21). Roseraie.

122. Abbaye de Chaalis, Fontaine-Chaalis, near Ermenonville, Oise. Rose-covered dome.
123. Abbaye de Chaalis, Fontaine-Chaalis, near Ermenonville, Oise. Birdbath in sea of old-fashioned roses.

124. Musée Rodin in Paris, 7th arrondissement
(p. 22).View across the reflecting pool and gardens
toward the museum, formerly known as Hotel Biron.
125. Musée Rodin in Meudon, Villa des Brillants,
Meudon, Hauts-de-Seine (p. 22). The Thinker.

pp. 146, 147
126, 127. Rose garden in Rueil-Malmaison, Hauts-
de-Seine (p. 22). Roseraie designed by Jules
Graveraux to feature the rose collection from
Josephine Bonaparte's uniquely rose garden.

128. Rose garden in L'Haÿ-les-Roses, Val-de-Marne (p. 22). Rose-fronted museum and café.
129. Rose garden in L'Haÿ-les-Roses, Val-de-Marne. Bust of Jules Graveraux, creator of original rose garden and grantor of his estate to the French government.

Jules GRAVEREAUX
(1844 - 1916)
CRÉATEUR DE LA ROSERAIE

130. Rose garden in L'Haÿ-les-Roses, Val-de-Marne. Rose-covered archway.
131. Rose garden in L'Haÿ-les-Roses, Val-de-Marne. Lattice-walled sculpture gallery.

132. Rose garden in Bagatelle, Bois de Boulogne,
16th arrondissement (p. 22). Roseraie.
133. Bagatelle, Bois de Boulogne, 16th arrondissement. Chinoiserie reflecting in lily pond.

134. Bagatelle, Bois de Boulogne, 16th arrondissement. Statue of faun near garden house.
135. Rose garden in Bagatelle, Bois de Boulogne,
16th arrondissement. View from gazebo.

136. Albert-Kahn, musée et jardins, Boulogne-Billancourt, Hauts-de-Seine (p. 22). Conservatory.
137. Albert-Kahn, musée et jardins, Boulogne-Billancourt, Hauts-de-Seine. Japanese garden ornament.
138. Albert-Kahn, musée et jardins, Boulogne-Billancourt, Hauts-de-Seine. Japanese tea room.

139. Albert-Kahn, musée et jardins, Boulogne-
Billancourt, Hauts-de-Seine. Stone-crafted wall.
140. Albert-Kahn, musée et jardins, Boulogne-
Billancourt, Hauts-de-Seine. Red bridge and rock-
work.

141. Parc de la Villette, 19th arrondissement (p. 23).
Canal and ferry dock.

146. Parc de Belleville, 20th arrondissement
(p. 23). Veil of waterfall as seen from behind.
147. Parc de Belleville, 20th arrondissement.
Topiary-accented walkway.

148. Promenade plantée, 12th arrondissement
(p. 23). Hanging gardens.
149. Promenade plantée, 12th arrondissement.
Green-edged stairway.
150. Promenade plantée, 12th arrondissement.
Elevated way through buildings.

151. Promenade plantée, 12th arrondissement.
Vine-covered tunnel over footpath.
152. Promenade plantée, 12th arrondissement.
Canopied walkway.

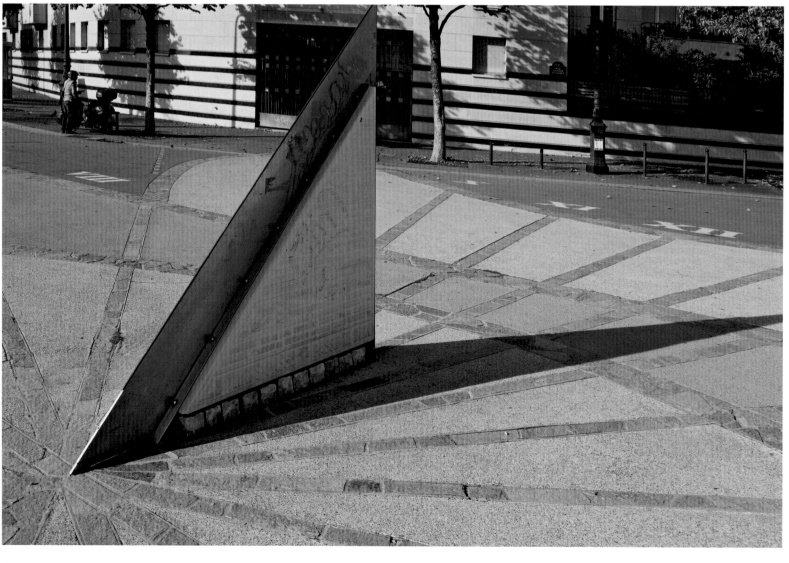

153. Jardin de Reuilly, 12th arrondissement (p. 23). Sundial.
154. Jardin de Reuilly, 12th arrondissement. Pedestrian suspension bridge.

155. Parc de Bercy, 12th arrondissement (p. 24).
Fountain and grass-roofed stadium.

156–158. Parc de Bercy, 12th arrondissement.
Three views of the fountain.

159. Parc de Bercy, 12th arrondissement. Wisteria-covered pillared arbor.
160. Parc de Bercy, 12th arrondissement. Pedestrian bridge linking two sides of the park.
161. Parc de Bercy, 12th arrondissement. Grape arbors referencing former use as wine warehousing district.

pp. 180/181
162. Parc André-Citroën, 15th arrondissement (p. 24). Oak-canopied walkway.
163. Parc André-Citroën, 15th arrondissement. Squared arches with wisteria vines.

164. Jardin Atlantique, 15th arrondissement (p. 24). Suspended over the Montparnasse railroad station; wave and water theme.
165. Jardin Atlantique, 15th arrondissement. Fountain wall.
166. Jardin Atlantique, 15th arrondissement. Tennis courts over areas too shallow to be landscaped.

167. Musée du quai Branly, 7th arrondissement, by Jean Nouvel (p. 24). Pathway in museum gardens.
168. Musée du quai Branly, 7th arrondissement, by Jean Nouvel. Vertical gardens.

169. Parc Clichy-Batignolles Martin Luther King,
17th arrondissement (p. 24). Floating staircase design to facilitate drainage.
170. Parc Clichy-Batignolles Martin Luther King,
17th arrondissement. Wave-edged sidewalk.

171. Parc Clichy-Batignolles Martin Luther King,
17th arrondissement. Engineered wetlands.
172. Parc Clichy-Batignolles Martin Luther King,
17th arrondissement. Windmill that advances the
park's goals of sustainability.

173. Parc Georges-Brassens, 15th arrondissement
(p. 24). Pond.
174. Parc Georges-Brassens, 15th arrondissement.
Pavilion.
175. Parc Georges-Brassens, 15th arrondissement.
Entry gates.